FIFTH EDITION

1B

GRAMMAR *in* CONTEXT

SANDRA N. ELBAUM

The cover photo shows the Leonard P. Zakim Bunker Hill Bridge over the Charles River in Boston, Massachusetts.

HEINLE
CENGAGE Learning™

Australia • Brazil • Japan • Korea • Mexico • Singapore • Spain • United Kingdom • United States

HEINLE
CENGAGE Learning™

Grammar in Context 1B, Student Book
Fifth Edition
Sandra N. Elbaum

Publisher: Sherrise Roehr

Acquisitions Editor: Tom Jefferies

Associate Development Editor:
  Sarah Sandoski

Director of Global Marketing: Ian Martin

Director of US Marketing: Jim McDonough

Product Marketing Manager: Katie Kelley

Marketing Manager: Caitlin Driscoll

Content Project Manager: Andrea Bobotas

Senior Print Buyer: Susan Spencer

Project Manager: Chrystie Hopkins

Production Services: Nesbitt Graphics, Inc.

Interior Design and Cover Design:
  Muse Group, Inc.

Library of Congress Control Number: 2009936997

ISBN 13: 978-1-4240-8089-2

ISBN 10: 1-4240-8089-4

Heinle
20 Channel Center Street
Boston, Massachusetts 02210
USA

Cengage Learning is a leading provider of customized learning solutions with office locations around the globe, including Singapore, the United Kingdom, Australia, Mexico, Brazil, and Japan Locate our local office at international.cengage.com/region

Cengage Learning products are represented in Canada by Nelson Education, Ltd.

Visit Heinle online at **elt.heinle.com**

Visit our corporate website at **www.cengage.com**

Printed in the United States of America.
1 2 3 4 5 6 7 8 9 10 — 13 12 11 10 09

Contents

Lesson 3

Lesson 4

Lesson 5

Lesson 6

Lesson 7

Lesson 8

Lesson 9

Lesson 10

Lesson 11

Lesson 12

Lesson 13

Lesson 14

Appendices

Index

Acknowledgments

Many thanks to Dennis Hogan, Sherrise Roehr, and Tom Jefferies from Heinle Cengage for their ongoing support of the *Grammar in Context* series. I would especially like to thank my development editor, Sarah Sandoski, for her patience, sensitivity, keen eye to detail, and invaluable suggestions.

And many thanks to my students at Truman College, who have increased my understanding of my own language and taught me to see life from another point of view. By sharing their observations, questions, and life stories, they have enriched my life enormously.

This new edition is dedicated to the millions of displaced people in the world. The U.S. is the new home to many refugees, who survived unspeakable hardships in Burundi, Rwanda, Sudan, Burma, Bhutan, and other countries. Their resiliency in starting a new life and learning a new language is a tribute to the human spirit.—*Sandra N. Elbaum*

Heinle would like to thank the following people for their contributions:

Elizabeth A. Adler-Coleman
Sunrise Mountain High
  School
Las Vegas, NV

Judith A. G. Benka
Normandale Community
  College
Bloomington, MN

Carol Brutza
Gateway Community
  College
New Haven, CT

Lyn Buchheit
Community College of
  Philadelphia
Philadelphia, PA

Charlotte M. Calobrisi
Northern Virginia
  Community College
Annandale, VA

Gabriela Cambiasso
Harold Washinton College
Chicago, IL

Jeanette Clement
Duquesne University
Pittsburgh, PA

Allis Cole
Shoreline Community
  College
Shoreline, WA

Fanshen DiGiovanni
Glendale Community
  College
Glendale, CA

Rhonda J. Farley
Cosumnes River College
Sacramento, CA

Jennifer Farnell
University of Connecticut
  American Language
  Program
Stamford, CT

Gail Fernandez
Bergen Community College
Paramus, NJ

Abigail-Marie Fiattarone
Mesa Community College
Mesa, AZ

John Gamber
American River College
Sacramento, CA

Marcia Gethin-Jones
University of Connecticut
  American Language
  Program
Storrs, CT

Kimlee Buttacavoli Grant
The Leona Group, LLC
Phoenix, AZ

Shelly Hedstrom
Palm Beach Community
  College
Lake Worth, FL

Linda Holden
College of Lake County
Grayslake, IL

Sandra Kawamura
Sacramento City College
Sacramento, CA

Bill Keniston
Normandale Community
  College
Bloomington, MN

Michael Larsen
American River College
Sacramento, CA

Bea C. Lawn
Gavilan College
Gilroy, CA

Rob Lee
Pasadena City College
Pasadena, CA

Oranit Limmaneeprasert
American River College
Sacramento, CA

Linda Louie
Highline Community
  College
Des Moines, WA

Melanie A. Majeski
Naugatuck Valley
  Community College
Waterbury, CT

Maria Marin
De Anza College
Cupertino, CA

Michael I. Massey
Hillsborough Community
  College-Ybor City Campus
Tampa, FL

Marlo McClurg-Mackinnon
Consumnes River College
Sacramento, CA

Michelle Naumann
Elgin Community College
Elgin, IL

Debbie Ockey
Fresno, CA

Lesa Perry
University of Nebraska at
  Omaha
Omaha, NE

Herbert Pierson
St. John's University
New York City, NY

Dina Poggi
De Anza College
Cupertino, CA

Steven Rashba
University of Bridgeport
Bridgeport, CT

Mark Rau
American River College
Sacramento, CA

Maria Spelleri
State College of Florida
  Manatee-Sarasota
Venice, FL

Eva Teagarden
Yuba College
Marysville, CA

Nico Wiersema
Texas A&M International
  University
Laredo, TX

Susan Wilson
San Jose City College
San Jose, CA

A word from the author

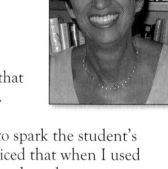

My parents immigrated to the U.S. from Poland and learned English as a second language. Born in the U.S., I often had the task as a child to explain the intricacies of the English language. It is no wonder that I became an English language teacher.

When I started teaching over forty years ago, grammar textbooks used a series of unrelated sentences with no context. I knew instinctively that there was something wrong with this technique. It ignored the fact that language is a tool for communication, and it missed an opportunity to spark the student's curiosity. As I gained teaching experience, I noticed that when I used interesting stories that illustrated the grammar students became more motivated, understood the grammar better, and used it more effectively.

In 1986, I published the first edition of *Grammar in Context* and have continued to search for topics that teach grammar in contexts that are relevant to students' lives. The contexts I've chosen each tell a story: practical ones about students' everyday experiences (such as renting an apartment) to inspirational ones about ordinary people doing extraordinary things (such as the pilot who landed his broken plane safely in the Hudson River). Whether the task is a fill-in grammar exercise, a listening activity, an editing exercise, an interactive conversation activity, or free writing, the context is reinforced throughout the lesson.

I hope you enjoy the new edition of *Grammar in Context*!

Sandra N. Elbaum

In memory of
Herman and Ethel Elbaum

Welcome to *Grammar in Context,*
Fifth Edition

Grammar in Context presents grammar in interesting contexts that are relevant to students' lives and then recycles the language and context throughout every activity. Learners gain knowledge and skills in both the grammar structures and topic areas.

The new fifth edition of *Grammar in Context* engages learners with updated readings, clear and accessible grammar explanations, and a new full-color design.

New To This Edition!

Full-color design makes grammar more visually contextualized and even easier to study and teach from.

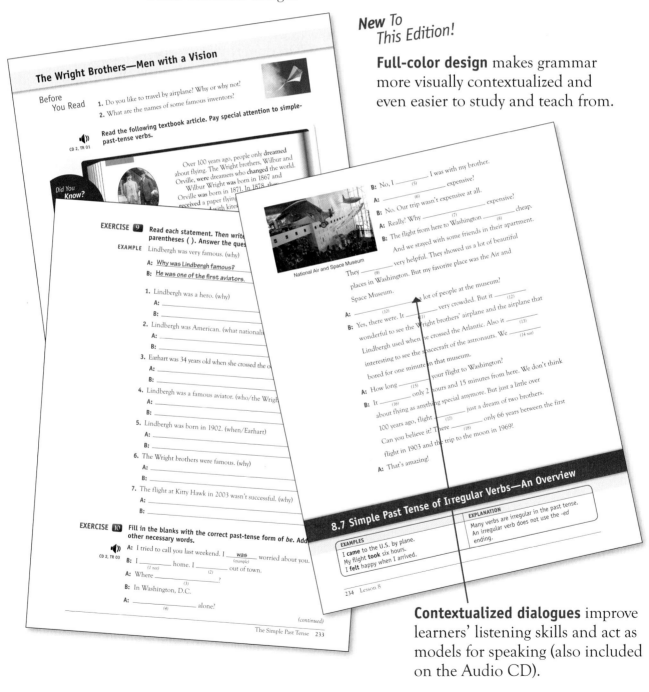

Contextualized dialogues improve learners' listening skills and act as models for speaking (also included on the Audio CD).

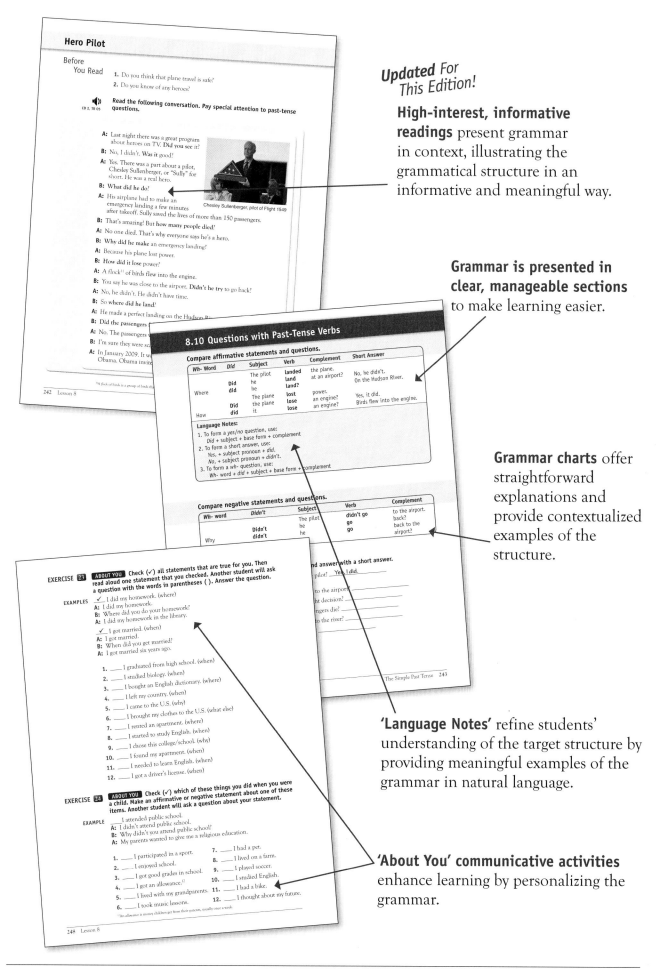

Hero Pilot

Before You Read
1. Do you think that plane travel is safe?
2. Do you know of any heroes?

🔊 CD 2, TR 05
Read the following conversation. Pay special attention to past-tense questions.

A: Last night there was a great program about heroes on TV. **Did you see** it?
B: No, I didn't. **Was it** good?
A: Yes. There was a part about a pilot, Chesley Sullenberger, or "Sully" for short. He was a real hero.
B: **What did he do?**
A: His airplane had to make an emergency landing a few minutes after takeoff. Sully saved the lives of more than 150 passengers.
B: That's amazing! But **how many people died?**
A: No one died. That's why everyone says he's a hero.
B: **Why did he make** an emergency landing?
A: Because his plane lost power.
B: **How did it lose** power?
A: A flock¹¹ of birds flew into the engine.
B: You say he was close to the airport. **Didn't he try** to go back?
A: No, he didn't. He didn't have time.
B: So **where did he land?**
A: He made a perfect landing on the Hudson R...
B: **Did the passengers** ...
A: No. The passengers ...
B: I'm sure they were sc...
A: In January 2009. It w...
    Obama. Obama invite...

Chesley Sullenberger, pilot of Flight 1549

¹¹A flock of birds is a group of birds fl...

242   Lesson 8

Updated *For This Edition!*

High-interest, informative readings present grammar in context, illustrating the grammatical structure in an informative and meaningful way.

Grammar is presented in clear, manageable sections to make learning easier.

8.10 Questions with Past-Tense Verbs

Compare affirmative statements and questions.

Wh- Word	Did	Subject	Verb	Complement	Short Answer
	Did	The pilot	landed	the plane.	
		he	land		No, he didn't.
Where	did	he	land?	at an airport?	On the Hudson River.
	Did	The plane	lost	power.	Yes, it did.
		the plane	lose	an engine?	Birds flew into the engine.
How	did	it	lose	an engine?	

Language Notes:
1. To form a *yes/no* question, use:
   Did + subject + base form + complement
2. To form a short answer, use:
   Yes, + subject pronoun + *did*.
   No, + subject pronoun + *didn't*.
3. To form a *wh-* question, use:
   Wh- word + *did* + subject + base form + complement

Compare negative statements and questions.

Wh- word	Didn't	Subject	Verb	Complement
		The pilot	didn't go	to the airport.
	Didn't	he	go	back?
Why	didn't	he	go	back to the airport?

Grammar charts offer straightforward explanations and provide contextualized examples of the structure.

...and answer with a short answer.

...pilot?   Yes, I did. _____

...to the airport? _____
...ght decision? _____
...ngers die? _____
...to the river? _____

The Simple Past Tense   243

EXERCISE 23 **ABOUT YOU** Check (✓) all statements that are true for you. Then read aloud one statement that you checked. Another student will ask a question with the words in parentheses ( ). Answer the question.

EXAMPLES
✓ I did my homework. (where)
A: I did my homework.
B: Where did you do your homework?
A: I did my homework in the library.

✓ I got married. (when)
A: I got married.
B: When did you get married?
A: I got married six years ago.

1. ____ I graduated from high school. (when)
2. ____ I studied biology. (when)
3. ____ I bought an English dictionary. (where)
4. ____ I left my country. (when)
5. ____ I came to the U.S. (why)
6. ____ I brought my clothes to the U.S. (what else)
7. ____ I rented an apartment. (where)
8. ____ I started to study English. (when)
9. ____ I chose this college/school. (why)
10. ____ I found my apartment. (when)
11. ____ I needed to learn English. (when)
12. ____ I got a driver's license. (when)

EXERCISE 24 **ABOUT YOU** Check (✓) which of these things you did when you were a child. Make an affirmative or negative statement about one of these items. Another student will ask a question about your statement.

EXAMPLE
____ I attended public school.
A: I didn't attend public school.
B: Why didn't you attend public school?
A: My parents wanted to give me a religious education.

1. ____ I participated in a sport.
2. ____ I enjoyed school.
3. ____ I got good grades in school.
4. ____ I got an allowance.¹²
5. ____ I lived with my grandparents.
6. ____ I took music lessons.
7. ____ I had a pet.
8. ____ I lived on a farm.
9. ____ I played soccer.
10. ____ I studied English.
11. ____ I had a bike.
12. ____ I thought about my future.

¹²An allowance is money children get from their parents, usually once a week.

248   Lesson 8

'Language Notes' refine students' understanding of the target structure by providing meaningful examples of the grammar in natural language.

'About You' communicative activities enhance learning by personalizing the grammar.

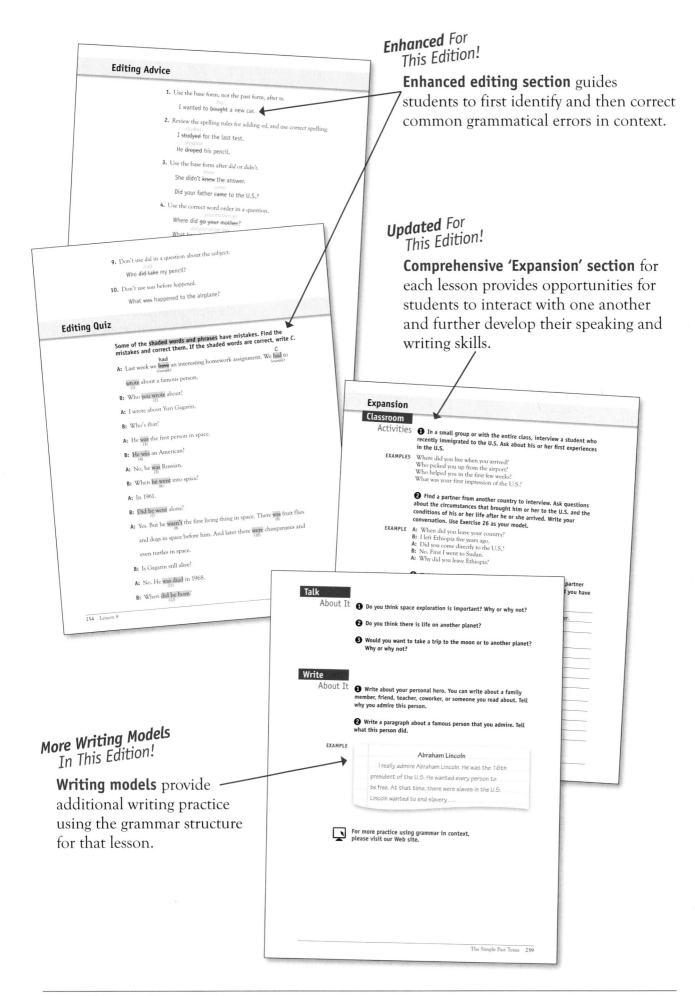

Enhanced For This Edition!

Enhanced editing section guides students to first identify and then correct common grammatical errors in context.

Updated For This Edition!

Comprehensive 'Expansion' section for each lesson provides opportunities for students to interact with one another and further develop their speaking and writing skills.

More Writing Models In This Edition!

Writing models provide additional writing practice using the grammar structure for that lesson.

Editing Advice

1. Use the base form, not the past form, after *to*.
   buy
   I wanted to ~~bought~~ a new car.

2. Review the spelling rules for adding *-ed*, and use correct spelling.
   studied
   I ~~studyed~~ for the last test.
   dropped
   He ~~droped~~ his pencil.

3. Use the base form after *did* or *didn't*.
   know
   She didn't ~~knew~~ the answer.
   come
   Did your father ~~came~~ to the U.S.?

4. Use the correct word order in a question.
   your mother go
   Where did ~~go your mother~~?
   What ...

9. Don't use *did* in a question about the subject.
   took
   Who ~~did take~~ my pencil?

10. Don't use *was* before *happened*.
    What ~~was~~ happened to the airplane?

Editing Quiz

Some of the shaded words and phrases have mistakes. Find the mistakes and correct them. If the shaded words are correct, write C.

had   C
A: Last week we ~~have~~ an interesting homework assignment. We had to
   (example)   *(example)*

   wrote about a famous person.
   (1)

B: Who you wrote about?
   (2)

A: I wrote about Yuri Gagarin.

B: Who's that?

A: He was the first person in space.
   (3)

B: He was an American?
   (4)

A: No, he was Russian.
   (5)

B: When he went into space?
   (6)

A: In 1961.

B: Did he went alone?
   (7)

A: Yes. But he wasn't the first living thing in space. There was fruit flies
   (8)   (9)

   and dogs in space before him. And later there were chimpanzees and
   (10)

   even turtles in space.

B: Is Gagarin still alive?

A: No. He was died in 1968.
   (11)

B: When did he born?
   (12)

254   Lesson 8

Expansion

Classroom Activities

❶ In a small group or with the entire class, interview a student who recently immigrated to the U.S. Ask about his or her first experiences in the U.S.

EXAMPLES   Where did you live when you arrived?
           Who picked you up from the airport?
           Who helped you in the first few weeks?
           What was your first impression of the U.S.?

❷ Find a partner from another country to interview. Ask questions about the circumstances that brought him or her to the U.S. and the conditions of his or her life after he or she arrived. Write your conversation. Use Exercise 26 as your model.

EXAMPLE   A: When did you leave your country?
          B: I left Ethiopia five years ago.
          A: Did you come directly to the U.S.?
          B: No. First I went to Sudan.
          A: Why did you leave Ethiopia?

Talk About It

❶ Do you think space exploration is important? Why or why not?

❷ Do you think there is life on another planet?

❸ Would you want to take a trip to the moon or to another planet? Why or why not?

Write About It

❶ Write about your personal hero. You can write about a family member, friend, teacher, coworker, or someone you read about. Tell why you admire this person.

❷ Write a paragraph about a famous person that you admire. Tell what this person did.

EXAMPLE

Abraham Lincoln

I really admire Abraham Lincoln. He was the 16th president of the U.S. He wanted every person to be free. At that time, there were slaves in the U.S. Lincoln wanted to end slavery . . .

For more practice using grammar in context, please visit our Web site.

The Simple Past Tense   259

FOR THE STUDENT:

New To This Edition!

- Online Workbook features additional exercises that learners can access in the classroom, language lab, or at home.

- Audio CD includes all readings and dialogues from the student book.

- Student Web site features additional practice: http://elt.heinle.com/grammarincontext

FOR THE TEACHER:

New To This Edition!

- Online Lesson Planner is perfect for busy instructors, allowing them to create and customize lesson plans for their classes, then save and share them in a range of formats.

Updated For This Edition!

- Assessment CD-ROM with ExamView® lets teachers create and customize tests and quizzes easily and includes many new contextualized test items.

- Teacher's Edition offers comprehensive teaching notes including suggestions for more streamlined classroom options.

- Instructor Web site includes a printable Student Book answer key.

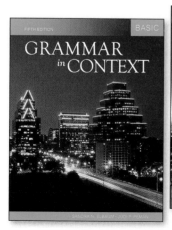 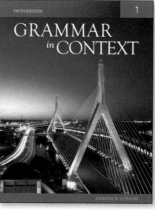 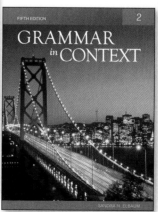 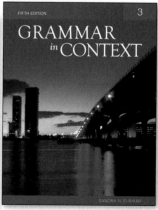

Grammar
The Simple Past Tense

Context
Flying

The Wright Brothers—Men with a Vision

Before You Read

1. Do you like to travel by airplane? Why or why not?

2. What are the names of some famous inventors?

CD 2, TR 01

Read the following textbook article. Pay special attention to simple-past-tense verbs.

Wilbur Wright, 1867–1912;
Orville Wright, 1871–1948

Over 100 years ago, people only **dreamed** about flying. The Wright brothers, Wilbur and Orville, **were** dreamers who **changed** the world.

Wilbur Wright **was** born in 1867 and Orville **was** born in 1871. In 1878, they **received** a paper flying toy from their father. They **played** with kites and **started** to think about the possibility of flight.

When they were older, they **started** a bicycle business. They **used** the bicycle shop to design their airplanes. They **studied** three aspects of flying: lift, control, and power. In 1899, they **constructed** their first flying machine—a kite made of wood, wire, and cloth. It **had** no pilot. Because of wind, it was difficult to control. They **continued** to study aerodynamics.[1] Finally Wilbur **designed** a small machine with a gasoline engine. Wilbur **tried** to fly the machine, but it **crashed**. They **fixed** it and **flew** it for the first time on December 17, 1903, with Orville as the pilot. The airplane **remained** in the air for twelve seconds. It **traveled** a distance of 120 feet. This historic flight **changed** the world. However, only four newspapers in the U.S. **reported** this historic moment.

The Wright brothers **offered** their invention to the U.S. government, but the government **rejected**[2] their offer at first. The government **didn't believe** that these men **invented** a flying machine. Finally, President Theodore Roosevelt **investigated** their claims and **offered** the inventors a contract to build airplanes for the U.S. Army.

December 17, 2003, **marked** 100 years of flight. There **was** a six-day celebration at Kitty Hawk, North Carolina, the location of the first flight. A crowd of 35,000 people **gathered** to see a replica[3] of the first plane fly. The cost to re-create the plane **was** $1.2 million. However, it **rained** hard that day and the plane **failed** to get off the ground.

You can now see the Wright brothers' original airplane in the Air and Space Museum in Washington, D.C.

[1]*Aerodynamics* is the branch of mechanics that deals with the motion of air and its effect on things.
[2]*Reject* means not accept.
[3]A *replica* is a copy of an original.

8.1 The Simple Past Tense of Regular Verbs

EXAMPLES	EXPLANATION
The Wright brothers **started** a bicycle business. They **dreamed** about flying. They **designed** an airplane. The president **offered** them a contract.	To form the simple past tense of regular verbs, we add -ed to the base form. **Base Form** **Past Form** start start**ed** dream dream**ed** design design**ed** offer offer**ed** The past form is the same for all persons.
The Wright brothers **wanted** to *fly*. They **continued** to *study* aerodynamics.	The verb after *to* does **not** use the past form.
The Wright brothers **invented** the airplane over 100 years **ago**. We **celebrated** the 100th anniversary of flight a few years **ago**.	We often use *ago* in sentences about the past. *Ago* means *before now*.

EXERCISE 1   **Read more about the Wright brothers. Underline the past tense verbs in the following sentences.**

EXAMPLE   The Wright brothers <u>lived</u> in Dayton, Ohio.

1. Their father worked as a Christian minister.
2. The boys learned mechanical things quickly.
3. They loved bicycles.
4. They opened the Wright Cycle Company repair shop, where they repaired bicycles.
5. They started to produce their own bicycle models.
6. The first airplane weighed over 600 pounds.
7. They succeeded in flying the first airplane in 1903.
8. Wilbur died nine years later, of typhoid.[4]
9. Orville lived to be 76 years old.

---

[4]*Typhoid* is a serious infection causing a fever and often death.

8.2 Spelling of the Past Tense of Regular Verbs

RULE	BASE FORM	PAST FORM
Add *-ed* to most regular verbs.	start rain	start**ed** rain**ed**
When the base form ends in *e*, add *-d* only.	die live	die**d** live**d**
When the base form ends in a consonant + *y*, change *y* to *i* and add *-ed*.	carry study	carr**ied** stud**ied**
When the base form ends in a vowel + *y*, add *-ed*. Do not change the *y*.	stay enjoy	stay**ed** enjoy**ed**
When a one-syllable verb ends in a consonant-vowel-consonant, double the final consonant and add *-ed*.	stop hug	stop**ped** hug**ged**
Do not double a final *w* or *x*.	show fix	show**ed** fix**ed**
When a two-syllable verb ends in a consonant-vowel-consonant, double the final consonant and add *-ed* only if the last syllable is stressed.	occúr permít	occur**red** permit**ted**
When the last syllable of a two-syllable verb is not stressed, do not double the final consonant.	ópen óffer	open**ed** offer**ed**

EXERCISE **2** **Write the past tense of these regular verbs. (Accent marks show you where a word is stressed.)**

EXAMPLES   learn __learned__   clap __clapped__

              love __loved__   lísten __listened__

1. play _____
2. study _____
3. decide _____
4. want _____
5. like _____
6. show _____
7. look _____
8. stop _____
9. háppen _____
10. carry _____

11. enjoy _____
12. drag _____
13. drop _____
14. start _____
15. follow _____
16. prefér _____
17. like _____
18. mix _____
19. admít _____
20. propél _____

8.3 Pronunciation of *-ed* Past Forms

PRONUNCIATION	RULE	EXAMPLES	
/t/	Pronounce /t/ after voiceless sounds: /p, k, f, s, š, č/	jump—jumped cook—cooked cough—coughed	kiss—kissed wash—washed watch—watched
/d/	Pronounce /d/ after voiced sounds: /b, g, v, đ, z, ž, ǰ, m, n, ŋ, l, r/ and all vowel sounds.	rub—rubbed drag—dragged love—loved bathe—bathed use—used massage—massaged charge—charged	name—named learn—learned bang—banged call—called care—cared free—freed
/əd/	Pronounce /əd/ after /d/ or /t/ sounds.	wait—waited hate—hated want—wanted	add—added decide—decided

EXERCISE 3 Go back to Exercise 2 and pronounce the base form and past form of each verb.

EXERCISE 4 Fill in the blanks with the past tense of the verb in parentheses ( ). Use the correct spelling.

EXAMPLE The Wright brothers _____received_____ a flying toy from their father.
(receive)

1. They _____ with kites.
(play)

2. They _____ about flying.
(dream)

3. They _____ everything they could about flying.
(study)

4. They _____ a bicycle business.
(start)

5. They _____ the bicycle shop to design airplanes.
(use)

6. They _____ to fly their first plane in 1899.
(try)

7. Their first plane _____.
(crash)

8. They _____ it.
(fix)

9. In 1903, their plane _____ in the air for 12 seconds.
(stay)

10. They _____ their invention to the U.S. government.
(offer)

11. The government _____ to offer them a contract.
(decide)

(continued)

12. Wilbur Wright _____ in 1912.
                    (die)

13. Orville Wright _____ for many more years.
                  (live)

14. Their invention _____ the world.
                  (change)

Charles Lindbergh and Amelia Earhart

Before You Read

1. When was the first time you traveled by airplane?

2. Do you recognize the people in the photos below?

CD 2, TR 02

Read the following textbook article. Pay special attention to the past-tense forms of *be*.

Charles Lindbergh,
1902–1974

At the beginning of the twentieth century, flight **was** new. It **was** not for everyone. It **was** only for the brave and adventurous. Two adventurers **were** Charles Lindbergh and Amelia Earhart.

Charles Lindbergh loved to fly. He **was** born in 1902, one year before the Wright brothers' historic flight. In 1927, a man offered a $25,000 reward for the first person to fly from New York to Paris nonstop. Lindbergh **was** a pilot for the United States Mail Service at that time. He wanted to win the prize.

He became famous because he **was** the first person to fly alone across the Atlantic Ocean. His plane **was** in the air for 33 hours. The distance of the flight **was** 3,600 miles. There **were** thousands of people in New York to welcome him home. He **was** an American hero. He **was** only 25 years old.

Another famous American aviator[5] **was** Amelia Earhart. She **was** the first woman to fly across the Atlantic Ocean alone. She **was** 34 years old. Americans **were** in love with Earhart. In 1937, however, she **was** on a flight around the world when her plane disappeared somewhere in the Pacific Ocean. No one really knows what happened to Earhart.

Amelia Earhart,
1897–1937

[5]*Aviator* means pilot.

8.4 Past Tense of *Be*

The verb *be* has two forms in the past: *was* and *were*.

EXAMPLES			EXPLANATION
Subject	*Was*	**Complement**	*I*
I		interested in the story.	*He*
Charles		a pilot.	*She*
He		brave.	*It* } was
Amelia	**was**	a pilot too.	singular subject
She		popular.	
The airplane		new in 1903.	
It		in the air for 12 seconds.	
Subject	*Were*	**Complement**	*We*
We		interested in the story.	*You*
You		in class yesterday.	*They* } were
Amelia and Charles	**were**	brave.	plural subject
They		adventurous.	
There	*Was*	**Singular Subject**	*There* + *was* + singular noun
There	**was**	a celebration in 2003.	
There	*Were*	**Plural Subject**	*There* + *were* + plural noun
There	**were**	thousands of people.	
Charles Lindbergh **was not** the first person to fly. We **were not** at the 2003 celebration.			To make a negative statement, put *not* after *was* or *were*.
I **wasn't** here yesterday. You **weren't** in class yesterday.			The contraction for *was not* is *wasn't*. The contraction for *were not* is *weren't*.

EXERCISE 5 **Fill in the blanks with *was* or *were*.**

EXAMPLE   Lindbergh and Earhart ____were____ very famous.

1. The Wright brothers _____ the inventors of the airplane.

2. The first airplane _____ in the air for 12 seconds.

3. Lindbergh and Earhart _____ aviators.

4. There _____ thousands of people in New York to welcome Lindbergh home.

5. Earhart _____ the first woman to fly across the Atlantic Ocean.

6. I _____ interested in the story about Earhart and Lindbergh.

7. _____ you surprised that a woman was a famous aviator?

8. Lindbergh _____ in Paris.

9. We _____ happy to read about flight.

10. There _____ a celebration of 100 years of flight in 2003.

11. There _____ thousands of people at the celebration.

8.5 Uses of *Be*

EXAMPLES	EXPLANATION
Lindbergh **was** an aviator.	Classification of the subject
Lindbergh **was** brave.	Description of the subject
Lindbergh **was** in Paris.	Location of the subject
Earhart **was** from Kansas.	Place of origin of the subject
She **was** born in 1897.	With *born*
There **were** thousands of people in New York to welcome Lindbergh.	With *there*
Lindbergh **was** 25 years old in 1927.	With age

EXERCISE **6** **Read each statement. Then write a negative statement with the words in parentheses ( ).**

EXAMPLE   The Wright brothers were inventors. (Earhart and Lindbergh)

<u>Earhart and Lindbergh weren't inventors.</u>

1. The train was common transportation in the early 1900s. (the airplane)

   _____

2. Earhart was from Kansas. (Lindbergh)

   _____

3. Lindbergh's last flight was successful. (Earhart's last flight)

   _____

4. Lindbergh's plane was in the air for many hours. (the Wright brothers' first plane)

   _____

5. The Wright brothers were inventors. (Earhart)

   _____

6. There were a lot of trains 100 years ago. (planes)

   _____

7. Lindbergh was born in the twentieth century. (the Wright brothers)

   _____

8. The 1903 flight at Kitty Hawk was successful. (the 2003 flight)

   _____

8.6 Questions with *Was/Were*

EXAMPLES	EXPLANATION

Was the first flight long?
    No, it **wasn't.**
Was the first flight successful?
    Yes, it **was.**
Were the Wright brothers inventors?
    Yes, they **were.**
	***Yes/No* Questions**
	    Was/were + subject . . . ?
	Short answers
	    Yes, + subject + *was/were.*
	    No, + subject + *wasn't/weren't.*

Were there a lot of people at the 100-year celebration?
    Yes, there **were.**
Was there a lot of rain that day?
    Yes, there **was.**
	***There* Questions**
	    Was/were + there . . . ?
	Short Answers
	    Yes, there *was/were.*
	    No, there *wasn't/weren't.*

How long **was** the first flight? Where **was** the first flight?	***Wh-* Questions** *Wh-* word + *was/were* + subject . . . ?
Why **wasn't** Amelia successful? Why **weren't** you there?	**Negative Questions** *Why* + *wasn't/weren't* + subject . . . ?

Who **was** with Earhart when she disappeared?
How many people **were** in the airplane?
	Subject Questions
	    Who + *was* . . . ?
	    How many . . . + *were* . . . ?

Compare affirmative statements and questions.

Wh- Word	*Was/Were*	Subject	*Was/Were*	Complement	Short Answer
		Amelia	was	born before 1903.	
	Was	she		born in the U.S.?	Yes, she was.
When	was	she		born?	In 1897.
		Charles and Amelia	were	famous.	
	Were	they		inventors?	No, they weren't.
		Someone	was	with Amelia.	
	Who		was	with Amelia?	A copilot.
		Many people	were	at the celebration.	
	How many people		were	at the celebration?	Thousands.

Compare negative statements and questions.

Wh- Word	*Wasn't/Weren't*	Subject	*Wasn't/Weren't*	Complement
		Air travel	**wasn't**	safe 100 years ago.
Why	**wasn't**	it		safe?
		The Wright brothers	**weren't**	afraid of flying.
Why	**weren't**	they		afraid?

EXERCISE 7 Read each statement. Then write a *yes/no* question with the words in parentheses ( ). Give a short answer.

EXAMPLE The Wright brothers were inventors. (Lindbergh)
Was Lindbergh an inventor? No, he wasn't.

1. The airplane was an important invention. (the telephone)

_____

2. Thomas Edison was an inventor. (the Wright brothers)

_____

3. Amelia Earhart was American. (Lindbergh)

_____

4. Travel by plane is common now. (100 years ago)

_____

5. There were telephones 100 years ago. (airplanes)

_____

6. You are in class today. (yesterday)

_____

7. I was interested in the story about the aviators. (you)

_____

8. I wasn't born in the U.S. (you)

_____

EXERCISE 8 **ABOUT YOU** Interview a classmate who is from another country.

1. Where were you born?
2. Were you happy or sad when you left your country?
3. Who was with you on your trip?
4. Were you happy or sad when you arrived?
5. What was your first impression of your new home?
6. Were you tired when you arrived?
7. Who was at the airport to meet you?
8. How was the weather on the day you arrived?

EXERCISE 9 **Read each statement. Then write a *wh-* question with the words in parentheses ( ). Answer the question.**

EXAMPLE Lindbergh was very famous. (why)

A: Why was Lindbergh famous?

B: He was one of the first aviators.

1. Lindbergh was a hero. (why)

   A: _____

   B: _____

2. Lindbergh was American. (what nationality/Earhart)

   A: _____

   B: _____

3. Earhart was 34 years old when she crossed the ocean. (how old/Lindbergh)

   A: _____

   B: _____

4. Lindbergh was a famous aviator. (who/the Wright brothers)

   A: _____

   B: _____

5. Lindbergh was born in 1902. (when/Earhart)

   A: _____

   B: _____

6. The Wright brothers were famous. (why)

   A: _____

   B: _____

7. The flight at Kitty Hawk in 2003 wasn't successful. (why)

   A: _____

   B: _____

EXERCISE 10 **Fill in the blanks with the correct past-tense form of *be*. Add any other necessary words.**

CD 2, TR 03

A: I tried to call you last weekend. I ___was___ worried about you.
(example)

B: I _____ home. I _____ out of town.
(1 not)   (2)

A: Where _____?
(3)

B: In Washington, D.C.

A: _____ alone?
(4)

(continued)

National Air and Space Museum

B: No, I _____. I was with my brother.

(5)

A: _____ expensive?

(6)

B: No. Our trip wasn't expensive at all.

A: Really? Why _____ expensive?

(7)

B: The flight from here to Washington _____ cheap.

(8)
And we stayed with some friends in their apartment.

They _____ very helpful. They showed us a lot of beautiful

(9)

places in Washington. But my favorite place was the Air and

Space Museum.

A: _____ a lot of people at the museum?

(10)

B: Yes, there were. It _____ very crowded. But it _____

(11) (12)
wonderful to see the Wright brothers' airplane and the airplane that

Lindbergh used when he crossed the Atlantic. Also it _____

(13)
interesting to see the spacecraft of the astronauts. We _____

(14 not)
bored for one minute in that museum.

A: How long _____ your flight to Washington?

(15)

B: It _____ only 2 hours and 15 minutes from here. We don't think

(16)
about flying as anything special anymore. But just a little over

100 years ago, flight _____ just a dream of two brothers.

(17)
Can you believe it? There _____ only 66 years between the first

(18)
flight in 1903 and the trip to the moon in 1969!

A: That's amazing!

8.7 Simple Past Tense of Irregular Verbs—An Overview

EXAMPLES	EXPLANATION
I **came** to the U.S. by plane. My flight **took** six hours. I **felt** happy when I arrived.	Many verbs are irregular in the past tense. An irregular verb does not use the -ed ending.

Robert Goddard

Before You Read

1. Did you ever see the first moon landing in 1969?
2. Are you interested in astronauts and rockets?

CD 2, TR 04

Read the following textbook article. Pay special attention to past-tense verbs.

Robert Goddard with early rocket, 1926

Robert Goddard **was** born in 1882. When he **was** a child, he **became** interested in firecrackers and **thought** about the possibility of space travel. He later **became** a physics professor at a university. In his free time, he **built** rockets and **took** them to a field, but they **didn't fly**. When he **went** back to his university after his failed attempts, the other professors **laughed** at him.

In 1920, Goddard **wrote** an article about rocket travel. He **believed** that one day it would be possible to go to the moon. When *The New York Times* **saw** his article, a reporter **wrote** that Goddard **had** less knowledge about science than a high school student. Goddard **wanted** to prove that *The New York Times* **was** wrong.

In 1926, he **built** a ten-foot rocket, **put** it into an open car, and **drove** to his aunt's nearby farm. He **put** the rocket in a field and **lit** the fuse. Suddenly the rocket **went** into the sky. It **traveled** at 60 miles per hour (mph) to an altitude of 41 feet. Then it **fell**

Astronaut Buzz Aldrin of Apollo 11 on the moon, 1969

into the field. The flight **lasted** 2½ seconds, but Goddard **was** happy about his achievement. Over the years, his rockets **grew** to 18 feet and **flew** to 9,000 feet in the air. No one **made** fun of him after he was successful.

When Goddard **died** in 1945, his work **did not stop**. Scientists **continued** to build bigger and better rockets. In 1969, when the American rocket Apollo 11 **took** the first men to the moon, *The New York Times* **wrote**: *"The Times regrets[6] the error."*

---

[6]*Regret* means to be sorry for.

8.8 List of Irregular Past Tense Verbs[7]

VERBS WITH NO CHANGE		FINAL *d* CHANGES TO *t*	
bet—bet	hurt—hurt	bend—bent	send—sent
cost—cost	let—let	build—built	spend—spent
cut—cut	put—put	lend—lent	
fit—fit	quit—quit		
hit—hit	shut—shut		

VERBS WITH A VOWEL CHANGE			
feel—felt	lose—lost	bring—brought	fight—fought
keep—kept	mean—meant[8]	buy—bought	teach—taught
leave—left	sleep—slept	catch—caught	think—thought
break—broke	steal—stole	begin—began	sing—sang
choose—chose	speak—spoke	drink—drank	sink—sank
freeze—froze	wake—woke	ring—rang	swim—swam
dig—dug	spin—spun	drive—drove	shine—shone
hang—hung	win—won	ride—rode	write—wrote
blow—blew	grow—grew	bleed—bled	meet—met
draw—drew	know—knew	feed—fed	read—read[9]
fly—flew	throw—threw	lead—led	
sell—sold	tell—told	find—found	wind—wound
shake—shook	mistake—mistook	lay—laid	pay—paid
take—took		say—said[10]	
tear—tore	wear—wore	bite—bit	hide—hid
		light—lit	
become—became	eat—ate	fall—fell	hold—held
come—came			
give—gave	lie—lay	run—ran	see—saw
forgive—forgave		sit—sat	
forget—forgot	get—got	stand—stood	
shoot—shot		understand—understood	

MISCELLANEOUS CHANGES			
be—was/were	go—went	hear—heard	
do—did	have—had	make—made	

[7]For an alphabetical list of irregular verbs, see Appendix D.
[8]There is a change in the vowel sound. *Meant* rhymes with *sent*.
[9]The past form of *read* is pronounced like the color *red*.
[10]*Said* rhymes with *bed*.

EXERCISE 11   **Read the following facts about the history of rockets. Underline the verbs. Write *R* for a regular verb. Write *I* for an irregular verb.**

EXAMPLE   Goddard <u>published</u> a paper on rockets in 1920. **R**

1. Goddard built and flew rockets from 1926 to 1939.
2. Germany used the first rockets in World War II in 1944.
3. The Russians launched their first satellite, Sputnik 1, in 1957.
4. The Americans sent up their first satellite, Explorer 1, in 1958.
5. Yuri Gagarin, a Russian, became the first person in space in 1961.
6. Alan Shepard, an American, went into space in 1961.
7. The United States put the first men on the moon in 1969.
8. A spacecraft on Mars transmitted color photos to Earth in 2004.

EXERCISE 12   **Fill in the blanks with the past tense of one of the words from the box below.**

fly	think	drive	be	fall
write	put	become ✓	see	

EXAMPLE   Goddard __*became*__ interested in rockets when he was a child.

1. He _____ a professor of physics.
2. People _____ that space travel was impossible.
3. Goddard _____ his first rocket in a car and _____ to his aunt's farm.
4. The rocket _____ for 2½ seconds and then it _____ to the ground.
5. Goddard never _____ the first moon landing.
6. *The New York Times* _____ about their mistake 49 years later.

EXERCISE 13   **Fill in the blanks with the past tense of the verb in parentheses ( ).**

EXAMPLE   The Wright brothers' father __*gave*__ them a flying toy.

(give)

1. They _____ a dream of flying.

(have)
2. They _____ interested in flying after seeing a flying toy.

(become)
3. They _____ many books on flight.

(read)

(continued)

4. They _____ bicycles.
   (sell)

5. They _____ the first airplane.
   (build)

6. At first they _____ problems with wind.
   (have)

7. They _____ some changes to the airplane.
   (make)

8. They _____ for the first time in 1903.
   (fly)

9. Only a few people _____ the first flight.
   (see)

10. President Theodore Roosevelt _____ about their airplane.
   (hear)

11. The airplane was an important invention because it _____
   (bring)

   people from different places closer together.

12. Thousands of people _____ to North Carolina for the 100th
   (go)

   anniversary of flight.

8.9 Negative Forms of Past Tense Verbs

Compare affirmative (A) and negative (N) statements with past-tense verbs.

EXAMPLES	EXPLANATION
A. Lindbergh **returned** from his last flight. **N.** Earhart **didn't return** from her last flight.	For the negative past tense, we use *didn't* + the base form for ALL verbs, regular and irregular.
A. The Wright brothers **flew** in their airplane. **N.** Goddard **didn't fly** in his rocket.	**Compare:** returned—didn't return flew—didn't fly
A. Goddard **built** rockets. **N.** He **didn't build** airplanes.	built—didn't build put—didn't put
A. The Russians **put** a woman in space in 1963. **N.** The Americans **didn't put** a woman in space until 1983.	**Remember:** *Put* and a few other past-tense verbs are the same as the base form.

EXERCISE 14 **Fill in the blanks with the negative form of the underlined words.**

EXAMPLE   Goddard <u>believed</u> in space flight. Other people _____ *didn't believe* _____ in space flight at that time.

1. The Wright brothers <u>dreamed</u> about flying. They
   _____ about rockets.

2. They <u>sold</u> bicycles. They _____ cars.

3. Their 1903 airplane <u>had</u> a pilot. Their first airplane
   _____ a pilot.

4. The Wright brothers <u>wanted</u> to show their airplane to the U.S.
   government. The government _____ to see it at first.

5. The Wright brothers <u>built</u> the first airplane. They
   _____ the first rocket.

6. Goddard <u>thought</u> his ideas were important. His colleagues
   _____ his ideas were important.

7. He <u>wanted</u> to build rockets. He _____ to build
   airplanes.

8. In 1920, a newspaper <u>wrote</u> that he was foolish. The newspaper
   _____ about the possibility of rocket travel.

9. In 1926 his rocket <u>flew</u>. Before that time, his rockets
   _____.

10. The first rocket <u>stayed</u> in the air for 2½ seconds. It
    _____ in the air for a long time.

11. Goddard <u>saw</u> his rockets fly. He _____ rockets go to
    the moon.

12. In 1957, the Russians <u>put</u> the first man in space. The Americans
    _____ the first man in space.

13. In 1969, the first Americans <u>walked</u> on the moon. Russians
    _____ on the moon.

14. A rocket <u>went</u> to the moon in 1969. A rocket _____
    to the moon during Goddard's lifetime.

EXERCISE 15 **ABOUT YOU** If you came to the U.S. from another country, fill in the blanks with the affirmative or negative form of the verb in parentheses to tell about the time before you came to the U.S. Add some specific information to tell more about each item.

EXAMPLES   I ___**studied**___ English before I came to the U.S. **I studied with a**
(study)

private teacher for three months.

OR

I ___**didn't study**___ English before I came to the U.S. **I didn't have**
(study)

enough time.

1. I _____ my money for dollars before I came to
(exchange)

the U.S.

2. I _____ a passport.
(get)

3. I _____ for a visa.
(apply)

4. I _____ English.
(study)

5. I _____ my furniture.
(sell)

6. I _____ goodbye to my friends.
(say)

7. I _____ an English dictionary.
(buy)

8. I _____ a clear idea about life in the U.S.
(have)

9. I _____ afraid about my future.
(be)

10. I _____ to another country first.
(go)

11. I _____ English well.
(understand)

12. I _____ a lot about American life.
(know)

EXERCISE **16** **ABOUT YOU** If you come from another city or country, tell if these things happened or didn't happen after you moved to this city. Add some specific information to tell more about each item.

EXAMPLE   find an apartment

I found an apartment two weeks after I arrived in this city.

OR

I didn't find an apartment right away. I lived with my cousins for two months.

1. find a job
2. register for English classes
3. rent an apartment
4. buy a car
5. get a Social Security card

6. go to the bank
7. visit a museum
8. see a relative
9. buy clothes
10. get a driver's license

EXERCISE **17** **ABOUT YOU** Tell if you did or didn't do these things in the past week. Add some specific information to tell more about each item.

EXAMPLE   go to the movies

I went to the movies last weekend with my brother. We saw a great movie.

OR

I didn't go to the movies this week. I didn't have time.

1. use the Internet
2. write a letter
3. go to the library
4. do laundry
5. buy groceries
6. use a phone card

7. buy a magazine
8. work hard
9. look for a job
10. rent a DVD
11. send e-mail
12. read a newspaper

Hero Pilot

Before You Read

1. Do you think that plane travel is safe?

2. Do you know of any heroes?

🔊 CD 2, TR 05

Read the following conversation. Pay special attention to past-tense questions.

A: Last night there was a great program about heroes on TV. **Did you see** it?

B: No, I didn't. **Was it** good?

A: Yes. There was a part about a pilot, Chesley Sullenberger, or "Sully" for short. He was a real hero.

B: **What did he do?**

A: His airplane had to make an emergency landing a few minutes after takeoff. Sully saved the lives of more than 150 passengers.

Chesley Sullenberger, pilot of Flight 1549

B: That's amazing! But **how many people died?**

A: No one died. That's why everyone says he's a hero.

B: **Why did he make** an emergency landing?

A: Because his plane lost power.

B: **How did it lose** power?

A: A flock[11] of birds flew into the engine.

B: You say he was close to the airport. **Didn't he try** to go back?

A: No, he didn't. He didn't have time.

B: So **where did he land?**

A: He made a perfect landing on the Hudson River, next to New York City.

B: **Did the passengers fall** into the water?

A: No. The passengers waited on the wings for rescue.

B: I'm sure they were scared. **When did this happen?**

A: In January 2009. It was a week before the inauguration of President Obama. Obama invited him and his crew to attend the inauguration.

---

[11]A *flock* of birds is a group of birds that fly together.

8.10 Questions with Past-Tense Verbs

Compare affirmative statements and questions.

Wh- Word	Did	Subject	Verb	Complement	Short Answer
		The pilot	**landed**	the plane.	
	Did	he	**land**	at an airport?	No, he didn't.
Where	**did**	he	**land?**		On the Hudson River.
		The plane	**lost**	power.	
	Did	the plane	**lose**	an engine?	Yes, it did.
How	**did**	it	**lose**	an engine?	Birds flew into the engine.

Language Notes:

1. To form a *yes/no* question, use:
   Did + subject + base form + complement
2. To form a short answer, use:
   Yes, + subject pronoun + *did.*
   No, + subject pronoun + *didn't.*
3. To form a *wh-* question, use:
   Wh- word + *did* + subject + base form + complement

Compare negative statements and questions.

Wh- word	Didn't	Subject	Verb	Complement
		The pilot	**didn't go**	to the airport.
	Didn't	he	**go**	back?
Why	**didn't**	he	**go**	back to the airport?

EXERCISE 18   **Read the questions and answer with a short answer.**

EXAMPLE   Did you read about the pilot? ___Yes, I did.___

1. Did the pilot return to the airport? _____
2. Did he make the right decision? _____
3. Did any of the passengers die? _____
4. Did the plane go into the river? _____
5. Was the pilot brave? _____

EXERCISE 19 **ABOUT YOU** Use these questions to ask another student about the time when he or she lived in his or her native country.

1. Did you study English in your country?
2. Did you live in a big city?
3. Did you live with your parents?
4. Did you know a lot about the U.S.?
5. Did you finish high school?
6. Did you own a car?
7. Did you have a job?
8. Did you think about your future?
9. Were you happy?

EXERCISE 20 Read each statement. Write a *yes/no* question about the words in parentheses ( ). Write a short answer.

EXAMPLE The Wright brothers had a dream. (Goddard) (yes)
Did Goddard have a dream? Yes, he did.

1. Wilbur Wright died in 1912. (his brother) (no)

_____

2. The Wright brothers built an airplane. (Goddard) (no)

_____

3. Earhart loved to fly. (Lindbergh) (yes)

_____

4. Lindbergh crossed the ocean. (Earhart) (yes)

_____

5. Lindbergh worked for the U.S. Mail Service. (Earhart) (no)

_____

6. Lindbergh became famous. (Earhart) (yes)

_____

7. Earhart disappeared. (Lindbergh) (no)

_____

8. Lindbergh was born in the twentieth century. (Earhart) (no)

_____

9. Lindbergh won money for his flight. (the Wright brothers) (no)

_____

10. People didn't believe the Wright brothers at first. (Goddard) (no)

_____

11. The Wright brothers dreamed about flight. (Goddard) (yes)

_____

12. Sully made an emergency landing. (a safe landing) (yes)

_____

13. Birds flew into one engine. (both engines) (no)

_____

14. Sully was safe. (the passengers) (yes)

_____

EXERCISE **21**   **Fill in the blanks with the correct words.**

EXAMPLE   What kind of engine _did the first airplane have?_ _____?
The first airplane had a gasoline engine.

1. Where _____?
   The Wright brothers built their plane in their bicycle shop.
2. Why _____?
   The first plane crashed because of the wind.
3. Why _____ the
   first flight in 1903?
   Many newspapers didn't report it because no one believed it.
4. Where _____?
   Lindbergh worked for the U.S. Mail Service.
5. Why _____?
   He crossed the ocean to win the prize money.
6. How much money _____?
   He won $25,000.
7. How old _____ when he crossed the ocean?
   Lindbergh was 25 years old when he crossed the ocean.
8. Where _____?
   Earhart was born in Kansas.
9. Where _____?
   She disappeared in the Pacific Ocean.

(continued)

10. Why _____?
Nobody knows why Earhart didn't return.

11. When _____?
The first man walked on the moon in 1969.

12. Why _____ the first moon landing?
Goddard didn't see the first moon landing because he died in 1945.

13. Why _____?
Sully was a hero because he saved lives.

14. How many _____?
He saved 150 lives.

15. Why _____?
He didn't return to the airport because he didn't have time.

EXERCISE **22** **Read each statement. Then write a question with the words in parentheses ( ). Answer with a complete sentence. (The answers are at the bottom of page 247.)**

EXAMPLE The Wright brothers were born in the nineteenth century. (Where)

Where were they born?

They were born in Ohio.

1. The Wright brothers were born in the nineteenth century.
(When/Lindbergh)

_____

_____

2. Their father gave them a toy. (What kind of toy)

_____

_____

3. They had a shop. (What kind of shop)

_____

_____

4. They designed airplanes. (Where)

_____

_____

5. They flew their first plane in North Carolina. (When)

_____

_____

6. The first plane stayed in the air for a few seconds. (How many seconds)

_____

_____

7. The U.S. government didn't want to see the airplane at first. (Why)

_____

_____

8. The Wright brothers invented the airplane. (What/Goddard)

_____

_____

9. Goddard took his rocket to his aunt's farm. (Why)

_____

_____

10. People laughed at Goddard. (Why)

_____

_____

11. Sully landed his plane. (Where)

_____

_____

12. Sully received an invitation from the president. (When)

_____

_____

13. The president thanked him. (Where)

_____

_____

ANSWERS TO EXERCISE 22:

(1) 1902, (2) a flying toy, (3) a bicycle shop, (4) in their bicycle shop, (5) in 1903, (6) 12 seconds, (7) they didn't believe it, (8) the rocket, (9) to see if it would fly, (10) they didn't believe him (they thought he was a fool), (11) on the Hudson River in New York City, (12) in January 2009, (13) at the inauguration

EXERCISE 23 **ABOUT YOU** Check (✓) all statements that are true for you. Then read aloud one statement that you checked. Another student will ask a question with the words in parentheses ( ). Answer the question.

EXAMPLES

✓ I did my homework. (where)
A: I did my homework.
B: Where did you do your homework?
A: I did my homework in the library.

✓ I got married. (when)
A: I got married.
B: When did you get married?
A: I got married six years ago.

1. ____ I graduated from high school. (when)
2. ____ I studied biology. (when)
3. ____ I bought an English dictionary. (where)
4. ____ I left my country. (when)
5. ____ I came to the U.S. (why)
6. ____ I brought my clothes to the U.S. (what else)
7. ____ I rented an apartment. (where)
8. ____ I started to study English. (when)
9. ____ I chose this college/school. (why)
10. ____ I found my apartment. (when)
11. ____ I needed to learn English. (when)
12. ____ I got a driver's license. (when)

EXERCISE 24 **ABOUT YOU** Check (✓) which of these things you did when you were a child. Make an affirmative or negative statement about one of these items. Another student will ask a question about your statement.

EXAMPLE

____ I attended public school.
A: I didn't attend public school.
B: Why didn't you attend public school?
A: My parents wanted to give me a religious education.

1. ____ I participated in a sport.
2. ____ I enjoyed school.
3. ____ I got good grades in school.
4. ____ I got an allowance.[12]
5. ____ I lived with my grandparents.
6. ____ I took music lessons.
7. ____ I had a pet.
8. ____ I lived on a farm.
9. ____ I played soccer.
10. ____ I studied English.
11. ____ I had a bike.
12. ____ I thought about my future.

[12]An *allowance* is money children get from their parents, usually once a week.

8.11 Questions About the Subject

EXAMPLES			EXPLANATION
Subject	**Verb**	**Complement**	When we ask a question about the subject,
Someone	saved	the passengers.	we use the past-tense form, not the base
Who	saved	the passengers?	form. We don't use *did* in the question.
			Compare:
Something	happened	to Sully's plane.	Where **did** the pilot **land** the airplane?
What	happened	to Sully's plane?	Who **landed** the airplane?
A president	invited	Sully.	When **did** the accident **happen**?
Which president	invited	Sully?	What **happened**?

EXERCISE 25 Choose the correct words to answer these questions about the subject. (The answers are at the bottom of the page.)

EXAMPLE Who invented the airplane?
(the Wright brothers)/ Goddard / Lindbergh)

1. Which country sent the first rocket into space?
   (*the U.S. / China / Russia*)

2. Who walked on the moon in 1969?
   (*an American / a Russian / a Canadian*)

3. Who sent up the first rocket?
   (*the Wright brothers / Goddard / Lindbergh*)

4. Who disappeared in 1937?
   (*Earhart / Goddard / Lindbergh*)

5. Who won money for flying across the Atlantic Ocean?
   (*Earhart / Lindbergh / Goddard*)

6. Which president showed interest in the Wright brothers' airplane?
   (*T. Roosevelt / Lincoln / Wilson*)

7. Which newspaper said that Goddard was a fool?
   (*Chicago Tribune / The Washington Post / The New York Times*)

8. How many people died in Sully's emergency landing?
   (*150 / 10 / no one*)

ANSWERS TO EXERCISE 25:

(1) Russia, (2) an American, (3) Goddard, (4) Earhart, (5) Lindbergh, (6) T. Roosevelt, (7) *The New York Times*, (8) no one

EXERCISE 26 **ABOUT YOU** Read one of the *who* questions below. Someone will volunteer an answer. Then ask the person who answered "I did" a related question.

EXAMPLE **A:** Who went to the bank last week?

B: I did.

A: Why did you go to the bank?

B: I went there to buy a money order.

1. Who brought a dictionary to class today?
2. Who drank coffee this morning?
3. Who wrote a composition last night?
4. Who watched TV this morning?
5. Who came to the U.S. alone?
6. Who made an international phone call last night?
7. Who studied English before coming to the U.S.?
8. Who bought a newspaper today?

EXERCISE 27 Fill in the blanks in this conversation between two students about their past.

A: I _____was born_____ in Mexico. I _____
  (example: born)   *(1 come)*

to the U.S. ten years ago. Where _____ born?
                                                      (2 be)

B: In El Salvador. But my family _____ to Guatemala
                                                           (3 move)

when I _____ ten years old.
                (4 be)

A: Why _____ to Guatemala?
              (5 move)

B: In 1998, we _____ our home.
                        (6 lose)

A: What _____?
              (7 happen)

B: A major earthquake _____ my town. Luckily,
(8 hit)

my family was fine, but the earthquake _____
(9 destroy)

our home and much of our town. We _____
(10 go)

to live with cousins in Guatemala.

A: How long _____ in Guatemala?
(11 stay)

B: I stayed there for about three years. Then I _____
(12 come)

to the U.S.

A: What about your family? _____ to the U.S. with you?
(13 come)

B: No. They _____ until I _____ a job
(14 wait)   (15 find)

and _____ my money. Then I _____
(16 save)   (17 bring)

them here later.

A: My parents _____ with me either. But my older
(18 not/come)

brother did. I _____ to go to school as soon as I
(19 start)

_____.
(20 arrive)

B: Who _____ you while you were in school?
(21 support)

A: My brother _____.
(22)

B: I _____ to school right away because I
(23 not/go)

_____ to work. Then I _____
(24 have)   (25 get)

a grant and _____ to go to City College.
(26 start)

A: Why _____ City College?
(27 choose)

B: I chose it because it has a good ESL program.

A: Me too.

Summary of Lesson 8

The Simple Past Tense

1. *Be*

Was	Were
I He She It } was in Paris.	We You They } were in Paris.
There was a problem.	There were many problems.

	Was	Were
AFFIRMATIVE	He **was** in Poland.	They **were** in France.
NEGATIVE	He **wasn't** in Russia.	They **weren't** in England.
YES/NO QUESTION	**Was** he in Hungary?	**Were** they in Paris?
SHORT ANSWER	No, he **wasn't**.	No, they **weren't**.
WH- QUESTION	Where **was** he?	When **were** they in France?
NEGATIVE QUESTION	Why **wasn't** he in Russia?	Why **weren't** they in Paris?
SUBJECT QUESTION	Who **was** in Russia?	How many people **were** in France?

2. Other Verbs

	REGULAR VERB (*WORK*)	IRREGULAR VERB (*BUY*)
AFFIRMATIVE	She **worked** on Saturday.	They **bought** a car.
NEGATIVE	She **didn't work** on Sunday.	They **didn't buy** a motorcycle.
YES/NO QUESTION	**Did** she **work** in the morning?	**Did** they **buy** an American car?
SHORT ANSWER	Yes, she **did**.	No, they **didn't**.
WH- QUESTION	Where **did** she **work**?	What kind of car **did** they **buy**?
NEGATIVE QUESTION	Why **didn't** she **work** on Sunday?	Why **didn't** they **buy** an American car?
SUBJECT QUESTION	Who **worked** on Sunday?	How many people **bought** an American car?

Editing Advice

1. Use the base form, not the past form, after *to*.

           buy
I wanted to ~~bought~~ a new car.

2. Review the spelling rules for adding *-ed*, and use correct spelling.

    studied
I ~~studyed~~ for the last test.

    dropped
He ~~droped~~ his pencil.

3. Use the base form after *did* or *didn't*.

        know
She didn't ~~knew~~ the answer.

        come
Did your father ~~came~~ to the U.S.?

4. Use the correct word order in a question.

        your mother go
Where did ~~go your mother~~?

        did your sister buy
What ~~bought your sister~~?

5. Use *be* with *born*. (Don't add *-ed* to *born*.) Don't use *be* with *died*.

        was born
Her grandmother ~~borned~~ in Russia.

She ~~was~~ died in the U.S.

    was
Where ~~did~~ your grandfather born?

    did
Where ~~was~~ your grandfather died?

6. Check your list of verbs for irregular verbs.

    brought
I ~~bringed~~ my photos to the U.S.

    saw
I ~~seen~~ the accident yesterday.

7. Use *be* with age.

        was
My grandfather ~~had~~ 88 years old when he died.

8. Don't confuse *was* and *were*.

      were
Where ~~was~~ you yesterday?

9. Don't use *did* in a question about the subject.

took

Who ~~did take~~ my pencil?

10. Don't use *was* before *happened*.

What ~~was~~ happened to the airplane?

Editing Quiz

Some of the shaded words and phrases have mistakes. Find the mistakes and correct them. If the shaded words are correct, write C.

had   *C*

A: Last week we ~~have~~ an interesting homework assignment. We had to

      (example)   (example)

wrote about a famous person.

(1)

B: Who you wrote about?

(2)

A: I wrote about Yuri Gagarin.

B: Who's that?

A: He was the first person in space.

(3)

B: He was an American?

(4)

A: No, he was Russian.

(5)

B: When he went into space?

(6)

A: In 1961.

B: Did he went alone?

(7)

A: Yes. But he wasn't the first living thing in space. There was fruit flies

(8)   (9)

and dogs in space before him. And later there were chimpanzees and

(10)

even turtles in space.

B: Is Gagarin still alive?

A: No. He was died in 1968.

(11)

B: When did he born?

(12)

A: He born in 1934. He had only 34 years old when he died. He never see
     (13)   (14)   (15)   (16)
the moon landing. That was happened in 1969, one year before he died.
                        (17)   (18)

B: Who did walk on the moon first? I forgetted his name.
         (19)   (20)

A: That was Neil Armstrong.

B: How did Gagarin died?
                        (21)

A: He were in a plane crash.
         (22)

B: That's so sad.

A: Yes, it is. They named a town in Russia after him.
                       (23)

Lesson 8 Test/Review

PART 1   **Write the past tense of each verb.**

EXAMPLES   live ___*lived*___   feel ___*felt*___

1. eat _____	**11.** drink _____
2. see _____	**12.** build _____
3. get _____	**13.** stop _____
4. sit _____	**14.** leave _____
5. hit _____	**15.** buy _____
6. make _____	**16.** think _____
7. take _____	**17.** run _____
8. find _____	**18.** carry _____
9. say _____	**19.** sell _____
10. read _____	**20.** stand _____

PART 2   **Fill in the blanks with the negative form of the underlined verb.**

EXAMPLE   Lindbergh <u>worked</u> for the U.S. Mail Service. Earhart
_____*didn't work*_____ for the U.S. Mail Service.

1. There <u>were</u> trains in 1900. There _____ any airplanes.

2. The Wright brothers <u>flew</u> a plane in 1903. They
_____ a plane in 1899.

3. Charles Lindbergh <u>was</u> an aviator. He _____ a
president.

4. The Wright brothers <u>invented</u> the airplane. They _____
the telephone.

5. Wilbur Wright <u>died</u> of typhoid fever. He _____ in
a plane crash.

6. Lindbergh <u>went</u> to Paris. Earhart _____ to Paris.

7. Lindbergh <u>came</u> back from his flight. Earhart _____
back from her last flight.

8. Goddard <u>was born</u> in the nineteenth century. He
_____ in the twentieth century.

9. Goddard <u>built</u> a rocket. He _____ an airplane.

10. Sully <u>lost</u> one engine. He _____ both engines.

PART 3 **Read each statement. Write a _yes/no_ question about the words in parentheses ( ). Write a short answer.**

EXAMPLE Lindbergh crossed the ocean. (Earhart) (yes)
<u>**Did Earhart cross the ocean? Yes, she did.**</u>

1. Wilbur Wright became famous. (Orville Wright) (yes)

_____

2. Lindbergh was an aviator. (Goddard) (no)

_____

3. Lindbergh flew across the Atlantic Ocean. (Earhart) (yes)

_____

4. Lindbergh was born in the U.S. (Goddard) (yes)

_____

5. Goddard wrote about rockets. (the Wright brothers) (no)

_____

6. The Russians sent a man into space. (the Americans) (yes)

_____

7. Goddard died in 1945. (Wilbur Wright) (no)

_____

8. The U.S. put men on the moon in 1969. (Russia) (no)

_____

9. People laughed at Goddard's ideas in 1920. (in 1969) (no)

_____

10. Sully landed the airplane in the river. (safely) (yes)

_____

PART 4 **Write a _wh-_ question about the words in parentheses ( ). An answer is not necessary.**

EXAMPLE   The Wright brothers became famous for their first airplane. (why/Lindbergh)

**Why did Lindbergh become famous?**

1. Earhart was born in 1897. (when/Lindbergh)

_____

2. Lindbergh crossed the ocean in 1927. (when/Earhart)

_____

3. Lindbergh got money for his flight. (how much)

_____

4. Earhart wanted to fly around the world. (why)

_____

5. Many people saw Lindbergh in Paris. (how many people)

_____

6. Goddard's colleagues didn't believe his ideas. (why)

_____

7. Wilbur Wright died in 1912. (when/Orville Wright)

_____

8. A president examined Goddard's ideas. (which president)

_____

9. Sully lost an engine. (how)

_____

10. Someone made an emergency landing. (who)

_____

Expansion

Classroom Activities

1 In a small group or with the entire class, interview a student who recently immigrated to the U.S. Ask about his or her first experiences in the U.S.

EXAMPLES
Where did you live when you arrived?
Who picked you up from the airport?
Who helped you in the first few weeks?
What was your first impression of the U.S.?

2 Find a partner from another country to interview. Ask questions about the circumstances that brought him or her to the U.S. and the conditions of his or her life after he or she arrived. Write your conversation. Use Exercise 26 as your model.

EXAMPLE
A: When did you leave your country?
B: I left Ethiopia five years ago.
A: Did you come directly to the U.S.?
B: No. First I went to Sudan.
A: Why did you leave Ethiopia?

3 Finish these statements five different ways. Then find a partner and compare your sentences to your partner's sentences. Did you have any sentences in common?

EXAMPLE
When I was a child, _I didn't like to do my homework._
When I was a child, _my parents sent me to camp every summer._
When I was a child, _my nickname was "Curly."_

a. When I was a child, _____
When I was a child, _____
When I was a child, _____
When I was a child, _____
When I was a child, _____

b. Before I came to the U.S., _____
Before I came to the U.S., _____
Before I came to the U.S., _____
Before I came to the U.S., _____
Before I came to the U.S., _____

Talk
About It

❶ Do you think space exploration is important? Why or why not?

❷ Do you think there is life on another planet?

❸ Would you want to take a trip to the moon or to another planet? Why or why not?

Write
About It

❶ Write about your personal hero. You can write about a family member, friend, teacher, coworker, or someone you read about. Tell why you admire this person.

❷ Write a paragraph about a famous person that you admire. Tell what this person did.

EXAMPLE

Abraham Lincoln

I really admire Abraham Lincoln. He was the 16th president of the U.S. He wanted every person to be free. At that time, there were slaves in the U.S. Lincoln wanted to end slavery . . .

 For more practice using grammar in context, please visit our Web site.

Grammar
Infinitives

Modals

Imperatives

Context
Smart Shopping

9.1 Infinitives—An Overview

EXAMPLES	EXPLANATION
I want **to go** shopping. I need **to buy** a new DVD player. It's important **to compare** prices. It's not hard **to be** a good shopper.	An infinitive is *to* + the base form: *to go, to buy, to compare, to be*

Getting the Best Price

Before
You Read

1. Do you like to shop for new things such as TVs, DVD players, computers, and microwave ovens?

2. Do you try to compare prices in different stores before you buy an expensive item?

CD 2, TR 06

Read the following magazine article. Pay special attention to infinitives.

Are you planning **to buy** a new TV, digital camera, or DVD player? Of course you want **to get** the best price. Sometimes you see an item you like at one store and then go to another store **to compare** prices. If you find the same item at a higher price, you probably think it is necessary  **to go** back to the first store **to get** the lower price. But it usually isn't. You can simply tell the salesperson in the second store that you saw the item at a better price somewhere else. Usually the salesperson will try **to match**[1] the other store's price. However, you need **to prove** that you can buy it cheaper elsewhere.[2] The proof can be an advertisement from the newspaper. If you don't have an ad, the salesperson can call the other store **to check** the price. The salesperson doesn't want you **to leave** the store without buying anything. He wants his store **to make** money. Some salespeople are happy to call the other store **to check** the price.

What happens if you buy something and a few days later see it cheaper at another store? Some stores will give you the difference in price for a limited period of time (such as 30 days). It's important **to keep** the receipt **to show** when you bought the item and how much you paid.

Every shopper wants **to save** money.

[1]To *match* a price means to give you an equal price.
[2]*Elsewhere* means somewhere else, another place.

9.2 Verbs Followed by an Infinitive

We often use an infinitive after certain verbs.

EXAMPLES				EXPLANATION
Subject	**Verb**	**Infinitive**	**Complement**	We use an infinitive after these verbs:
I	plan	**to buy**	a camera.	begin hope prefer
We	want	**to get**	the best price.	continue like promise
You	need	**to be**	a smart shopper.	decide love start
She	likes	**to save**	money.	expect need try
				forget plan want
They	want	**to buy**	a DVD player.	An infinitive never has an ending. It never shows tense. Only the first verb has an ending or shows tense.
We	wanted	**to buy**	a new TV.	
He	is planning	**to buy**	a microwave oven.	*Wrong*: He wanted to *bought* a new TV.

Pronunciation Notes:

1. In informal speech, *want to* is pronounced "wanna." Listen to your teacher pronounce these sentences:

   I *want to* buy a DVD.

   Do you *want to* go shopping with me?

2. In other infinitives, we often pronounce *to* like "ta" (after a consonant sound), "da" (after a vowel sound), or "a" (after a "d" sound). Listen to your teacher pronounce these sentences:

   Do you like to watch movies at home? ("ta")

   I plan to buy a new DVD player. ("ta")

   Try to get the best price. ("da")

   We decided to buy a digital camera. ("a")

   I need to compare prices. ("a")

EXERCISE 1 **Fill in the blanks with an infinitive. Answers may vary.**

EXAMPLE   I want ___to buy___ a new TV.

1. I like _____ money.

2. I decided _____ about $500.

3. I want _____ the best price.

4. I forgot _____ the Internet before going to the stores.

5. I need _____ a smart shopper.

6. Some people prefer _____ online.

EXERCISE 2 **ABOUT YOU** Make a sentence about yourself with the words given. Use an appropriate tense. You may find a partner and compare your sentences to your partner's sentences.

EXAMPLES   like/eat
I like to eat pizza.

learn/speak
I learned to speak German when I was a child.

try/find
I'm trying to find a bigger apartment.

1. love/go
2. like/play
3. need/have
4. expect/get
5. want/go
6. plan/buy
7. need/understand
8. not need/have
9. try/learn

EXERCISE 3 **ABOUT YOU** Ask a question with the words given in the present tense. Another student will answer.

EXAMPLE   like/shop

A: Do you like to shop?
B: Yes, I do. OR No, I don't.

1. try/compare prices
2. plan/buy something new
3. like/shop alone
4. like/shop online
5. like/use coupons
6. try/get the best price

EXERCISE 4 **ABOUT YOU** Ask a question with "Do you want to . . . ?" or "Do you plan to . . . ?" and the words given. Another student will answer. Then ask a *wh-* question with the words in parentheses ( ) whenever possible.

EXAMPLE   buy a car (why)

A: Do you plan to buy a car?
B: Yes, I do.
A: Why do you want to buy a car?
B: I don't like public transportation.

1. take a computer course next semester (why)

2. move (why) (when)

3. leave this country (why) (when)

4. get a job/get another job (what kind of job)

5. become an American citizen (why)

6. transfer to a different school (why)

7. take another English course next semester (which course)

8. learn another language (which language)

9. review the last lesson (why)

9.3 *It* + *Be* + Adjective + Infinitive

We often use an infinitive with sentences beginning with an impersonal *it*.

It	*Be* (+ *not*)	Adjective	Infinitive Phrase	EXPLANATION
It	is	important	**to save** your receipt.	An infinitive can follow these adjectives:
It	is	easy	**to shop**.	dangerous hard good
It	isn't	necessary	**to go** back to the first store.	possible difficult expensive
				impossible easy boring
				important necessary nice

EXERCISE 5   Complete each statement.

EXAMPLE   It's expensive to own __a big car._____

1. It's important to learn _____
2. It's hard to pronounce _____
3. It's hard to lift _____
4. It's necessary to own _____
5. It's easy to learn _____
6. It's hard to learn _____
7. It isn't necessary to know _____

EXERCISE 6   Complete each statement with an infinitive phrase.

EXAMPLE   It's easy __to ride a bike._____

1. It's boring _____
2. It's impossible _____
3. It's possible _____
4. It's necessary _____
5. It's dangerous _____
6. It's hard _____
7. It isn't good _____
8. It isn't necessary _____

EXERCISE 7   Answer the following questions. (You may work with a partner and ask and answer with your partner.)

1. Is it important to be bilingual?
2. Is it important to know English in your native country?
3. Is it possible to find a job in the U.S. without knowing any English?
4. Is it easy to learn English grammar?
5. Is it dangerous to text while driving?
6. Is it necessary to have a computer?

9.4 *Be* + Adjective + Infinitive

We often use an infinitive after certain adjectives.

EXAMPLES				EXPLANATION
Subject	***Be***	**Adjective**	**Infinitive Phrase**	We can use an infinitive after these adjectives:
I	am	ready	**to buy** a camera.	
The salesman	is	glad	**to help** you.	happy afraid lucky
He	is	prepared	**to make** a sale.	sad prepared proud
				glad ready pleased

EXERCISE 8   ABOUT YOU Fill in the blanks.

EXAMPLE I'm ready _to do the exercise._____

1. I'm lucky _____
2. I'm proud _____
3. I'm happy _____
4. I'm sometimes afraid _____
5. I'm not afraid _____
6. I'm not prepared _____
7. I was sad _____

EXERCISE 9   ABOUT YOU Answer the following questions.

1. Are you happy to be in this country?
2. Are you afraid to make a mistake when you speak English?
3. Were you sad to leave your country?
4. Are you prepared to have a test on this lesson?
5. Are you happy to be a student at this school?
6. Are you afraid to walk alone at night?

9.5 Using an Infinitive to Show Purpose

EXAMPLES	EXPLANATION
I went to a store **to buy** a digital camera. I went to a second store **to compare** prices. The saleswoman called the first store **to check** the price.	We use an infinitive to show the purpose of an action. Do not use *for* to show purpose. *Wrong*: I went to a store *for buy* a digital camera.
I use a digital camera **to** e-mail photos to my friends. I use a digital camera **in order to** e-mail photos to my friends.	*To* for purpose is the short form of *in order to*.

EXERCISE **10** **Fill in the blanks to show purpose.**

EXAMPLE   I bought a phone card to ___call my friends._____

1. I use my dictionary to _____

2. He went to an appliance store in order to _____
   _____

3. She worked overtime in order to _____
   _____

4. I bought the Sunday newspaper to _____

5. You need to show your driver's license to _____
   _____

6. Some people join a health club in order to _____
   _____

7. On a computer, you use the mouse to _____

8. When you return an item to a store, take your receipt in order to _____
   _____

9. Shoppers use coupons in order to _____

10. Many people shop online to _____

EXERCISE **11** **Fill in the blanks to complete this conversation. Answers may vary.**

🔊
CD 2, TR 07

A: Do you want to see my new digital camera?

B: Wow. It's so small. Does it take good pictures?

A: Absolutely. I use this camera _____to take_____ all my pictures.
                                        (example)

B: Was it expensive?

A: Not really. I went online _____ prices. Then I
(1)

went to several stores in this city _____ the best price.
(2)

B: Do you take a lot of pictures?

A: Oh, yes. And I e-mail them to my family back home.

B: Do you ever make prints of your pictures?

A: Yes. I buy high-quality glossy paper _____ prints for
(3)

my family album.

B: Is it hard to use the camera?

A: At first I had to read the manual carefully _____
(4)

how to take good pictures and transfer them to my computer.

But now it's easy. I'll take a picture of you. Smile.

B: Let me see it. My eyes are closed in the picture. Take another picture

of me.

A: OK. This one's better. But I don't like the background. It's too dark.

I can use a photo-editing program _____ the color.
(5)

B: Can you use the program _____ me more handsome?
(6)

Getting A Customer's Attention

1. Do you try free samples of food in supermarkets?
2. Do you ever go to the movies early in the day to get a cheaper ticket?

CD 2, TR 08

Read the following magazine article. Pay special attention to objects before an infinitive.

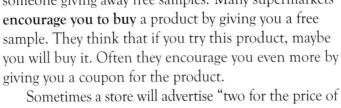

Stores use several techniques to get your business. Did you ever go to a food store and see someone giving away free samples? Many supermarkets **encourage you to buy** a product by giving you a free sample. They think that if you try this product, maybe you will buy it. Often they encourage you even more by giving you a coupon for the product.

Sometimes a store will advertise "two for the price of one." This is a marketing technique to get your interest. After you come into the store for the sale item, the manager **wants you to do** the rest of your shopping there too.

Movie theaters will lower their price in the early hours. This is because most people don't think of going to a movie early in the day. Both you and the movie theater benefit when you take advantage of the reduced price. You help fill the theater and get a cheap ticket in return.

Another way to get customer attention is with good service. Sometimes as you're leaving a store, a salesperson may ask you, "Do you **want me to take** this out to your car for you?" There is no extra charge for such service.

With so much competition between businesses, owners and managers have to use all kinds of techniques to get our attention and **encourage us to shop** at their store and return often.

9.6 Object Before an Infinitive

EXAMPLES	EXPLANATION
They **like you to try** the free samples. Do you **want me to carry** this out to your car for you? They **want us to do** all our shopping in one store. I **expect salespeople to be** courteous. I **expect them to be** helpful, too.	After *like, want, need, expect,* and *encourage,* we can use a noun or object pronoun (*me, you, him, her, it, us, them*) + an infinitive.

EXERCISE **12** **Circle the correct words in parentheses ( ) to complete each conversation.**

🔊 *Conversation 1*

CD 2, TR 09

Salesman: Do you want (*me* / *I*) (*to help* / *help*) you
(example)   (1)

find something?

Mother: Yes. We could use your help. Our daughter

wants (*we* / *us*) (*bought* / *to buy*) her a new
(2)   (3)

cell phone. We don't know which plan to buy.

Salesman: How many minutes a month does she talk on the phone?

Mother: She never stops talking on the phone. I want

(*her to use* / *that she use*) it just for emergencies, but she chats with
(4)

her friends all the time.

Salesman: Here's a plan I want (*you to consider* / *that you consider*).
(5)

It has unlimited calls at night and on weekends.

Mother: You don't understand. We want (*her* / *she*) to use the phone
(6)

less, not more.

Conversation 2

Man: I'm going to buy a digital camera on Saturday. I need

(*that you* / *you to*) come with me.
(1)

Friend: Why? How do you want (*that I* / *me to*) help you?
(2)

Man: You already have a digital camera, so you can give me advice.

Conversation 3

Husband: Oh, look. There's free food over there. Do you want

(*me to get* / *that I get*) you a little hot dog?
(1)

(*continued*)

Wife: No. They just want (*us / we*) to spend our money on things
(2)

we don't need.

Conversation 4

Grocery Clerk: Excuse me, miss. You have a lot of bags. Do you want

(*me / I*) (*to help / helping*) you take them to your car?
(1)   (2)

Shopper: Thanks. My husband's in the car. I wanted (*him / he*)
(3)

(*to help / helped*) me, but he hates shopping. He prefers
(4)

to wait in the car. Besides, he has a bad back, and I

don't want (*that he / him to*) lift anything. We're having a
(5)

dinner party on Saturday and we invited 20 guests, but I . . .

Grocery Clerk: Uh, excuse me. I hear my boss calling me. He needs

me now (*to give / giving*) him some help.
(6)

EXERCISE 13 **Two brothers are talking. Fill in the blanks with the first verb, an object pronoun, and the second verb.**

A: Mom and Dad say I spend too much money. They __expect me to save__
(example: expect/save)

my money for the future. I _____ me alone.
(1 want/leave)

B: You do? I thought you _____ you a car.
(2 wanted/buy)

A: Well, I do. You know how much I hate to take the bus. I

_____ to them for me. Tell them I need a car.
(3 want/talk)

B: I'm not going to do that. They are trying to _____
(4 encourage/be)

more responsible.

A: I *am* responsible.

B: No, you're not. Remember when you told Mom you wanted a

new MP3 player? You _____ it for you.
(5 expected/buy)

And remember when you lost your cell phone? You told Dad because

you _____ you a new one.
(6 wanted/buy)

A: Well, I'm still in school and I don't have much money.

B: Mom and Dad _____ and start to take

(7 expect/graduate)

responsibility for yourself. You buy too much stuff.

A: No, I don't. By the way, did I tell you I broke my camera?

9.7 Overview of Modals

LIST OF MODALS	FACTS ABOUT MODALS

can
 	
could
 	
should
 	
will
 	
would
 	
may
 	
might
 	
must
	1. Modals are different from other verbs because they don't have an *-s, -ed,* or *-ing* ending.
	    He **can** compare prices. (not: He *cans*)
	2. Modals are different from other verbs because we don't use an infinitive after a modal.[3] We use the base form.
	    COMPARE:
	    He **wants to buy** a digital camera.
	    He **might buy** a digital camera.
	3. To form the negative, put *not* after the modal.
	    You **should not** throw away the receipt.
	    Hurry! These prices **may not** last.
	4. Some verbs are like modals in meaning: *have to, be able to.*
	    You **must** return the item within 30 days. = You **have to** return the item within 30 days.
	    He **can't** get a credit card. = He **is not able to** get a credit card.

Compare affirmative statements and questions.

Wh- Word	Modal	Subject	Modal	Base Form	Complement	Short Answer
		You	should	buy	a new TV.	
	Should	you		buy	a DVD player?	No, you shouldn't.
What	should	you		buy?		
		Who	should	buy	a new TV?	
		She	can	compare	prices.	
	Can	she		compare	prices online?	Yes, she can.
How	can	she		compare	prices online?	
		Who	can	compare	prices?	

Compare negative statements and questions.

Wh- Word	Modal	Subject	Modal	Base Form	Complement
		He	shouldn't	buy	an expensive camera.
Why	shouldn't	he		buy	an expensive camera?

[3]Exception: *ought to. Ought to* means *should.*

Smart Shopping: Coupons, Rain Checks, and Rebates

**Before
You Read**

1. Do you see coupons in magazines and newspapers? Do you use them?
2. Do you see signs that say "rebate" on store products? Do you see signs that say "Buy one, get one free"?

| MANUFACTURER'S COUPON | DO NOT DOUBLE | EXPIRES 12/15/2011 |

Save 50¢

Tony T's
Homemade
Pizza Sauce

CONSUMER: Limit one coupon per purchase.
RETAILER: Please redeem for face value as specified. Any other use constitutes fraud.
Cash value: 1/100 cent.

4677000072

GTG
Good Time Grocery

No. 7942

Rain Check

Date _____ Item size _____
Item _____ Discount _____
Item quantity _____ Item Price _____ Expiration _____

Good toward similar item of equal or lesser value

Authorization _____

CD 2, TR 10

Read the following magazine article. Pay special attention to modals and related expressions.

Do you ever receive coupons in the mail?

Manufacturers often send coupons to shoppers. They want people to try their products. If you always use the same toothpaste and the manufacturer gives you a coupon for a different toothpaste, you **might** try the new brand.[4] Coupons have an expiration date. You **should** pay attention to this date because you **cannot** use the coupon after this date.

Rebate Form
Name
Address
City/State   Zip   Phone
Product name: _____
Size/Weight: _____
Price: _____
Store where purchased: _____
Date of purchase: _____
Proof of purchase attached: **yes / no**

Stores have weekly specials. But there is usually a limit. If you see a sign that says, "Eggs, $1.69 a dozen. Limit 2," this means you **can** buy only two dozen at this price. If you see a sign that says, "3 for $1.00," you **don't have to** buy three items to get the special price. If you buy only one, you **will** pay 34¢.

What **should** you do if a store has a special but you **can't** find this item on the shelf? If this item is sold out, you **can** go to the customer service desk and ask for a rain check. A rain check allows you to buy this item at the sale price even after the sale is over. A rain check usually has an expiration date. You **must** buy this item by the expiration date if you want to receive the sale price.

If you see a sign that says "rebate," this means that you **can** get money back from the manufacturer. You **have to** mail the proof of purchase and the cash register receipt to the manufacturer to prove that you bought this product. Also you **have to** fill out a small form. The manufacturer **will** return some money to you. It **may** take six to eight weeks to receive this money.

These sales techniques help manufacturers get your attention, but they also help you save money.

[4]The *brand* is the company name.

9.8 Can

EXAMPLES	EXPLANATION
I **can** find many ways to save money. I **can** explain how to use a rebate.	Ability
If you use coupons, you **can** save money. If the item is sold out, you **can** get a rain check.	Possibility
The sign says, "Eggs $1.69 a dozen. Limit 2." You **can** buy only two cartons of eggs at the special price. You **can** return an item within 30 days.	Permission
I **can't afford to** eat in a restaurant every day. **Can** you **afford** to buy steaks?	*Can afford to* means have enough money to buy something.
You **cannot** buy more than the limited quantity. You **can't** use a coupon after the expiration date.	The negative of *can* is *cannot*. The contraction is *can't*.

Pronunciation Notes:

1. In affirmative statements, we usually pronounce *can* /kən/. In negative statements, we pronounce *can't* /kænt/. Sometimes it is hard to hear the final **t**, so we must pay attention to the vowel sound and the stress to hear the difference between *can* and *can't*. Listen to your teacher pronounce these sentences:
   I *can* gó. /kən/
   I *cán't* go. /kænt/
2. In a short answer, we pronounce *can* /kæn/.
   Can you help me later?
   Yes, I *can*. /kæn/

EXERCISE 14 These sentences are true about an American supermarket. Check (✓) which ones are true about a supermarket in another country.

1. _____ You can use coupons.

2. _____ You can sometimes buy two items for the price of one.

3. _____ You can cash a check.

4. _____ You can buy stamps.

5. _____ You can get a rain check.

6. _____ You can pay by check or credit card.

7. _____ You can't bargain⁵ for the price.

8. _____ You can return an item if you're not satisfied. You can get your money back.

⁵To *bargain* for a price means to make an offer lower than the price the seller is asking.

(continued)

9. ____ You can get free bags (paper or plastic).

10. ____ You can use a shopping cart. Small children can sit in the cart.

11. ____ If you have a small number of items, you can go to a special lane.

12. ____ You can shop 24 hours a day (in some supermarkets).

EXERCISE `15` `ABOUT YOU` **Fill in the blanks with *can* or *can't* to tell about your abilities.**

EXAMPLE I ____*can*___ drive a car.

I ___*can't*___ fly a plane.

1. I _____ read without glasses.

2. I _____ speak Spanish.

3. I _____ drive a car.

4. I _____ play tennis.

5. I _____ sing well.

6. I _____ change a tire.

7. I _____ save money.

8. I _____ read the newspaper without a dictionary.

EXERCISE `16` `ABOUT YOU` **Ask a question about a classmate's abilities with the word(s) given. Another student will answer.**

EXAMPLE speak Spanish

A: Can you speak Spanish?
B: Yes, I can. OR No, I can't.

1. write with your left hand

2. type without looking at the keyboard

3. run fast

4. play chess

5. ski

6. play the piano

7. speak French

8. bake a cake

9. play the guitar

10. sew

EXERCISE `17` `ABOUT YOU` **Write down one thing that you can do well. Share your answer with a partner or with the entire class.**

_____

9.9 Should

EXAMPLES	EXPLANATION
You **should** use coupons to save money. What **should** I do if the item is sold out? You **should** compare prices before you buy.	We use *should* to give or ask for advice.
You **should not** waste your money. You **shouldn't** buy things you don't need.	The negative of *should* is *should not*. The contraction is *shouldn't*. We use the negative to give advice or a warning.

EXERCISE 18 If someone from another country is going to live in the U.S., what advice would you give him or her about shopping? Work with a partner to write six sentences of advice.

EXAMPLE   You should always look at the expiration date on a food product.

You should shop for summer clothes in July and August. Summer

clothes are cheapest at that time.

1. _____
2. _____
3. _____
4. _____
5. _____
6. _____

EXERCISE 19 Write a sentence to give advice in each of the following situations. Answers will vary.

EXAMPLE   The price of strawberries is high this week.

Maybe we shouldn't buy them this week.

1. I love this coffee. It's half price this week.

_____

2. I have a rain check for eggs. It expires tomorrow.

_____

3. I spent too much money on groceries last week.

_____

4. My supermarket gives you 10¢ for every bag you bring back.

_____

(continued)

5. I have ice cream in my bag, and it's a warm day today.

_____

6. My kids always want me to buy them sweets.

_____

7. I get coupons in the mail, but I always throw them away.

_____

EXERCISE 20 **A wife (W) and husband (H) are at the supermarket. Fill in the blanks with _should_ + a verb to complete the conversation. Answers may vary.**

CD 2, TR 11

W: _____Should we buy_____ ice cream? It's on sale.
   (example)

H: It's so hot today. And we have to stop at the dentist before we go home.

   We _____ it today. It'll melt.
   _(1)_

H: Look. Our favorite coffee is half price this week. _____
                                          _(2)_

   a bag?

W: We _____ a lot.
      _(3)_

H: How about candy for the kids? They always ask us for candy.

W: That's not a good idea. They _____ so much
                                _(4)_

   candy. It's not good for them. Where's our shopping list? We

   _____ our list and not buy things we don't need.
      _(5)_

   We _____ careful how we spend our money.
      _(6)_

H: You're right. Cheese is on our list. (_Husband picks up cheese._)

W: You _____ at the expiration date. This cheese has
        _(7)_

   tomorrow's date. We _____ fresher cheese. You
                      _(8)_

   almost never come shopping with me. You _____
                                        _(9)_

   with me more often. You can learn to be a better shopper.

H: You're right. Look. The sign says, "Bring your own bags. Get 10¢ for

   each bag." Next time we _____ our own bags. You see?
                         _(10)_

   I'm learning.

W: Great. _____ with a credit card or use cash?
            _(11)_

H: I've got enough cash on me. Let's use cash.

EXERCISE 21 Check (✓) if you agree or disagree about what schoolchildren should or shouldn't do. Discuss your answers with the whole class or in a small group.

	I agree.	I disagree.
1. Children should go to a teacher when they have a family problem.		
2. They shouldn't play video games.		
3. They should select their own TV programs.		
4. They shouldn't trust all adults.		
5. They should always tell the truth.		
6. They should be responsible for taking care of younger sisters and brothers.		
7. They should select their own friends.		
8. They should always obey their parents and teachers.		
9. They should learn to use a computer.		
10. They should study a foreign language.		
11. They should help their parents with small jobs in the house.		
12. They should learn about money when they're young.		

EXERCISE **22** **Read each statement. Then ask a question with the word(s) in parentheses ( ). Another student will answer.**

EXAMPLE The students should do the homework. (why)

      A: Why should they do the homework?
      B: It helps them understand the lesson.

1. The students should study the lessons. (why)
2. The teacher should take attendance. (when)
3. The students should bring their textbooks to class. (what else)
4. I should study modals. (why)
5. We should register for classes early. (why)
6. The teacher should speak clearly. (why)
7. The students shouldn't talk during a test. (why)
8. We shouldn't do the homework in class. (where)
9. The teacher should announce a test ahead of time. (why)

9.10 *Must*

EXAMPLES	EXPLANATION
To get a rebate, you **must** send the proof of purchase. You **must** include your receipt.	We use *must* to talk about rules and laws. *Must* has a very official, formal tone.
It's late. I **must** get to the store before it closes. We're almost out of milk!	We can use *must* for personal necessity. It shows a sense of urgency.
You **must not** use the handicapped parking space if you don't have permission. The store **mustn't** sell a product after its expiration date.	For the negative, use *must not*. The contraction is *mustn't*. *Must not* and *cannot* are very close in meaning. You *must not* park in the handicapped space = You *cannot* park in the handicapped space.

EXERCISE 23   **Here are some rules in a supermarket. Fill in the blanks with *must* or *must not*.**

1. Employees in the deli department _____ wear gloves.

2. Employees _____ touch food with their bare hands.

3. When employees use the washroom, they _____ wash their hands before returning to work.

4. The store _____ sell food after the expiration date.

5. Customers _____ take shopping carts out of the parking lot.

EXERCISE 24   **Name something. Discuss your answers.**

EXAMPLE   Name something you must have if you want to drive.
You must have a license.

1. Name something you must do or have if you want to leave the country.

2. Name something you must not carry onto an airplane.

3. Name something you must not do in the classroom.

4. Name something you must not do during a test.

5. Name something you must not do or have in your apartment.

6. Name something you must do or have to enter an American university.

7. Name something you must do when you drive a car.

9.11 Have To

	EXAMPLES	EXPLANATION
AFFIRMATIVE	I don't have enough milk. I **have to** go shopping. If you want to return an item, you **have to** show a receipt.	*Have to* is similar in meaning to *must*. *Have to* is less formal. We use it for personal obligations.
NEGATIVE	A: The DVD player was cheaper in the first store. Let's go back there. B: You **don't have to** go back there. Just tell the salesperson, and she'll probably give you the same price. A: Can we sample those cookies? B: Sure. If we don't like them, we **don't have to** buy them.	*Don't have to* means it's not necessary. You have a choice.

EXERCISE 25 **ABOUT YOU** Tell if you *have to* or *don't have to* do these things at this school. (Remember: *don't have to* means it's not necessary.)

EXAMPLES study before a test
I have to study before a test.

study in the library
I don't have to study in the library. I can study at home.

1. wear a suit to school
2. come to class on time
3. stand up to ask a question in class
4. do homework
5. notify the teacher if I'm going to be absent
6. call the teacher "professor"
7. raise my hand to answer
8. take a final exam
9. wear a uniform
10. buy my own textbooks

EXERCISE 26 Ask your teacher what he or she *has to* or *doesn't have to* do.

EXAMPLE work on Saturdays

A: Do you have to work on Saturdays?
B: Yes, I do. OR No, I don't.

1. take attendance
2. give students grades
3. call students by their last names
4. wear a suit
5. work in the summer
6. have a master's degree
7. work on Saturdays
8. come to school every day

EXERCISE 27   **ABOUT YOU**   **If you are from another country, write four sentences about students and teachers in your country. Tell what they _have to_ or _don't have to_ do. Use the ideas from the previous exercises. You may share your sentences with a small group or with the class.**

EXAMPLE   <u>In my country, students have to wear a uniform.</u>

1. _____
2. _____
3. _____
4. _____

EXERCISE 28   **Tell what Judy _has to_ or _doesn't have to_ do in these situations. Answers may vary.**

EXAMPLE   Judy has a coupon for cereal. The expiration date is tomorrow.
She has to ___<u>use it by tomorrow or she won't get the discount.</u>___.

1. The coupon for cereal says "Buy 2, get 50¢ off."
   She has to _____ in order to get the discount.
2. Judy has no milk in the house.
   She has to _____ more milk.
3. Eggs are on sale for $1.69, limit two cartons. She has three cartons of eggs.
   She has to _____ one of the cartons of eggs.
4. She has a rebate application. She has to fill out the application if she wants to get money back.
   She also has to _____ the proof-of-purchase symbol and the receipt to the manufacturer.
5. She wants to pay by check. The cashier asks for her driver's license.
   She has to _____.
6. She has 26 items in her shopping cart. She can't go to a lane that says "10 items or fewer."
   She has to _____ another lane.

9.12 *Must* and *Have To*

**In affirmative statements, *have to* and *must* are very similar in meaning.
In negative statements, *have to* and *must* are very different in meaning.**

	EXAMPLES	EXPLANATION
AFFIRMATIVE	If you wish to return an item, you **must** have a receipt. You **must** send the rebate coupon by October 1. You **have to** send the rebate coupon by October 1.	Use *must* or *have to* for rules. *Must* is more formal or more official, but we can use *have to* for rules too.
	I don't have any milk. I **have to** go to the store to buy some. I need to buy a lot of things. I **have to** use a shopping cart.	Use *have to* for personal obligations or necessities.
NEGATIVE	You **must not** park in the handicapped parking space. The store **must not** sell an item after the expiration date.	*Must not* shows that something is prohibited or against the law.
	The sign says, "3 for $1.00," but you **don't have to** buy three to get the sale price. You **don't have to** pay with cash. You can use a credit or debit card.	*Don't have to* shows that something is not necessary, that there is a choice.

EXERCISE **29** **Fill in the blanks with *must not* or *don't have to*.**

EXAMPLES   You _____must not_____ take a shopping cart out of the parking lot.

We _____don't have to_____ shop every day. We can shop once a week.

1. If you sample a product, you _____ buy it.

2. If you have just a few items, you _____ use a shopping cart. You can use a basket.

3. If you have a lot of items in your shopping cart, you

   _____ use the checkout that says "10 items or fewer."

4. You _____ park in the handicapped parking space if you don't have permission.

5. You _____ take your own bags to the supermarket. The cashier will give you bags for your groceries.

9.13 *Might/May* and *Will*

EXAMPLES	EXPLANATION

I have a coupon for a new toothpaste. I **might** buy it. I **may** like it.
 	
A rebate check **might** take six to eight weeks.
	May and *might* have the same meaning. They show possibility.
	
	Compare *maybe* (adverb) with *may* or *might* (modal verbs):
	  Maybe it *will* take eight weeks.
	  It *may* take eight weeks.
	  It *might* take eight weeks.

Those cookies taste great, but they **may not** be healthy for you. I **might not** have time to shop next week, so I'll buy enough for two weeks.	The negative of *may* is *may not*. The negative of *might* is *might not*. We do not make a contraction for *may not* and *might not*.
If the price is 3 for $1.00, you **will** pay 34¢ for one. If the sign says "Two for one," the store **will** give you one item for free.	*Will* shows certainty about the future.

EXERCISE 30 **Tell what may or might happen in the following situations. Answers may vary.**

EXAMPLE   Meg needs to go shopping. She's not sure what her kids want.

They might _____ **want a new kind of** _____ cereal.

1. She's not sure if she should buy the small size or the large size of cereal. The large size may _____ cheaper.

2. If she sends in the rebate form today, she might _____ a check in about six weeks.

3. The store sold all the coffee that was on sale. The clerk said, "We might _____ more coffee tomorrow."

4. Bananas are so expensive this week. If she waits until next week, the price may _____.

5. The milk has an expiration date of June 27. Today is June 27. She's not going to buy the milk because it might _____.

6. She's not sure what brand of toothpaste she should buy. She might buy the one she usually buys, or she might _____.

EXERCISE **31**   Tell what *may* or *might* happen in the following situations.
If you think the result is certain, use *will*.

EXAMPLES   If you don't put money in a parking meter, _you might get a ticket._

If you are absent from tests, _you may not pass the course._

If you don't pass the tests, _you'll fail the course._

1. If you drive too fast, _____

2. If you get a lot of tickets in one year, _____

3. If you don't water your plants, _____

4. If you don't take the final exam, _____

5. If you don't lock the door of your house, _____
_____

6. If you eat too much, _____

7. If you work hard and save your money, _____
_____

8. If the weather is nice this weekend, _____

9. If you park in the handicapped space without permission, _____
_____

9.14 Making Requests

EXAMPLES	EXPLANATION
Park over there. **Don't park** in the handicapped space. **Send** the rebate coupon soon. **Do not** wait.	We can use imperatives to make a request. The imperative is the base form of the verb. The subject is *you*, but we don't include *you* in the sentence. For a negative, put *don't* (or *do not*) before the verb.
May I see your driver's license? **Could** you give me change for a dollar?	We also use modals to make requests. Modals give the request a more polite tone.

The Customer Service Counter

Before You Read

1. Do you have a check-cashing card at a local supermarket?

2. Do you pay with cash when you shop in a supermarket?

CD 2, TR 12

Read the following conversation, first between two friends (A and B), and then between A and a customer service representative (C). Pay special attention to requests.

A: I need to cash a check.

B: **Let's go** to the customer service counter at Nick's. Someone told me they have a check-cashing service there.

A: **Could** you drive?

B: **Why don't we** walk? It's not far.

At the customer service counter:

C: **Can** I help you?

A: Yes. **I'd like** to cash a check.

C: Do you have a check-cashing card?

A: No, I don't.

C: Here's an application. Please **fill** it out.

A: I don't have a pen. **Could** I use your pen?

C: Here's a pen.

A: Thanks.

A few minutes later:

A: Here's my application.

C: **May** I see your driver's license?

A: Here it is. Did I fill out the application correctly?

C: No. Please **don't write** in the gray box. You made another mistake too. You wrote the day before the month. Please **write** the month before the day. For August 29, we write 8/29, not 29/8. **Why don't you fill out** another form? Here's a clean one.

A: Thanks.

(continued)

A few minutes later:

A: Here it is. **Could** you check to see if I filled it out right this time?

C: You forgot to sign your name. Please **sign** your name on the bottom line.

A: OK. **Could** you cash my check now?

C: I'm sorry, sir. We have to wait for approval. We'll send you your check-cashing card in the mail in a week to ten days. **Can** I help you with anything else?

A: Yes. **I'd like** to buy some stamps.

C: Here you are. Anything else?

A: No. That's it.

C: Have a nice day.

Nick's Fresh Values **Check Cashing Application**

For Office Use Only - Do Not Write In This Area	Card Number

NOTICE: This form must be submitted in person at our Customer Service Desk. Please be prepared to provide your Driver's License or State I.D. and Social Security number if you apply for check cashing privileges. Thank You.

CUSTOMER INFO

YOUR NAME — Ms. Mrs. Mr. — First — Middle Initial — Last

SOCIAL SECURITY NUMBER — DRIVER'S LICENSE NUMBER — STATE ISSUED

STREET ADDRESS — APT. NO. — CITY — STATE — ZIP CODE

AREA CODE — HOME PHONE NUMBER

COMPLETE ONLY IF 2 CARDS ARE REQUESTED — Card Number

SPOUSE INFO

SPOUSE'S NAME — Ms. Mrs. Mr. — First — Middle Initial — Last

SOCIAL SECURITY NUMBER — DRIVER'S LICENSE NUMBER — STATE ISSUED

I understand that when I present my Fresh Values Card, Nick's will keep a record of the products I purchase for its own internal use. I also understand that from time to time I may receive direct mail offers from Nick's which may contain valuable coupons, offers or samples. THE INFORMATION WHICH I PROVIDE NICK'S AND THE RECORDS OF THE PRODUCTS WHICH I PURCHASE WILL NOT BE SOLD OR GIVEN TO ANY THIRD PARTY. ☐ By checking this box, I am indicating that I do not wish to receive special mailings. Please present this card every time you shop at any Nick's store to receive your valuable discounts. This card remains the property of Nick's Finer Foods, Inc. and its privileges may be rescinded at any time.

COMPLETE THIS SECTION FOR CHECK CASHING PRIVILEGES

EMPLOYER INFO

YOUR EMPLOYER/PENSION PROVIDER — YOUR EMPLOYER'S PHONE NUMBER — HOW LONG

SPOUSE'S EMPLOYER — SPOUSE'S EMPLOYER'S PHONE NUMBER — HOW LONG

BANK INFO

BANK NAME — CITY — STATE — CHECKING ACCOUNT NUMBER — HOW LONG

Check Cashing Limits

CASH ☐ $300

GOVERNMENT* ☐ $500

PAYROLL* ☐ $500

* Must present check

I certify that the above information is correct to the best of my knowledge and authorize Nick's Finer Foods, Inc. to verify this information. I agree that my Fresh Values Card is for my personal use only and guarantee all checks cashed by use of this card. In the event of loss or theft of my card, I understand I am still responsible for all checks cashed with this card until its loss or theft is reported to Nick's Finer Foods. I agree to reimburse Nick's and/or its agents, for any returned checks and to pay any service fee, if applicable. For additional information on Nick's confidentiality agreement or check cashing terms and conditions, please see our information brochure.

SIGNATURE — Date

Spouse's Signature (If Applicable) — Date

NICK'S USE ONLY

☐ 1. NEW CUSTOMER CHECK CASHING   ☐ 2. REPLACEMENT CARD   ☐ 3. NEW CUSTOMER FV ONLY   ☐ 4. ADD CHECK CASHING

CURRENT CARD # — Store Number

VERIFIED BY

9.15 Imperatives

Imperatives give instructions, warnings, and suggestions.

EXAMPLES	EXPLANATION
Please **sign** your name at the bottom. **Write** the month before the day. **Be** careful when you fill out the application. **Don't write** in the gray box.	We use the imperative form to give instructions.
Stand up. **Walk, don't run!**	We use the imperative to give a command.
Watch out! There's a car coming! **Don't move.** There's a bee on your nose!	We use the imperative to give a warning.
Always do your best. **Never give** up.	We use the imperative to give encouragement. We can put *always* and *never* before an imperative.
Have a nice day. **Make** yourself at home.	We use the imperative in certain conversational expressions.
Go away. **Leave** me alone.	We use the imperative in some angry, impolite expressions.
Let's get an application for check cashing. **Let's not** make any mistakes.	*Let's* = *let us*. We use *let's* + the base form to make a suggestion. The negative form is *let's not*. *Let's* includes the speaker.

EXERCISE 32 Fill in the blanks with an appropriate imperative verb (affirmative or negative) to give instructions. Answers may vary.

EXAMPLE _____*Go*_____ to the customer service desk for an application.

1. _____ out the application in pen.

2. _____ a pencil to fill out an application.

3. _____ all the information in clear letters.

4. If you have a middle name, _____ your middle initial.

5. _____ anything in the box in the lower right corner.

6. If you are not married, _____ out the second part about spouse information.

7. When you give your telephone number, always _____ your area code.

8. _____ your last name before your first name on this application.

9. _____ the application to a person at the customer service counter.

EXERCISE `33` **Choose one of the activities from the following list. Use imperatives to give instructions on how to do the activity. (You may work with a partner.)**

EXAMPLE   get from school to your house

Take the number 53 bus north from the corner of Elm Street. Ask the driver for a transfer. Get off at Park Avenue. Cross the street and wait for a number 18 bus.

1. hang a picture
2. change a tire
3. fry an egg
4. prepare your favorite recipe
5. hem a skirt
6. write a check
7. make a deposit at the bank
8. tune a guitar
9. get a driver's license
10. use a washing machine
11. prepare for a job interview
12. get from school to your house
13. get money from a cash machine (automatic teller)
14. do a search on the Internet
15. send a text message

EXERCISE `34` **Work with a partner. Write a list of command forms that the teacher often uses in class. Read your sentences to the class.**

EXAMPLE   *Open your books to page 10.*

Don't come late to class.

1. _____
2. _____
3. _____
4. _____
5. _____

EXERCISE 35 **Fill in the blanks with an appropriate verb to complete this conversation.**

A: I need to cash a check.

B: We need to get some groceries. Let's ___*go*___ to the *(example)* supermarket.

A: Do you want to drive there?

B: The supermarket is not so far. Let's _____. *(1)*

A: It looks like rain.

B: No problem. Let's _____ an umbrella. *(2)*

A: Let's _____. It's late and the stores will close soon. *(3)*

B: Don't worry. This store is open 24 hours a day.

A: We're almost out of dog food. Let's _____ a *(4)* 20-pound bag.

B: Let's not _____ then. I don't want to carry a *(5)* 20-pound bag home. Let's _____ instead. *(6)*

EXERCISE 36 **Work with a partner. Write a few suggestions for the teacher or other students in this class using *let's* or *let's not*. Read your suggestions to the class.**

EXAMPLES Let's review verb tenses.

Let's not speak our native languages in class.

1. _____

2. _____

3. _____

4. _____

5. _____

6. _____

9.16 Using Modals to Make Requests and Ask Permission

An imperative form may sound too strong in some situations. Modals can make a request sound more polite.

EXAMPLES	EXPLANATION
Would / **Could** you cash my check, please?	We use these modals in a question to make a request. These forms are more polite than "Cash my check."
May / **Could** / **Can** I use your pen, please?	We use these modals in a question to ask permission. These forms are more polite than "Give me your pen."
I **would like** to cash a check. How **would** you **like** your change?	*Would like* has the same meaning as *want*. *Would like* is softer than *want*. The contraction of *would* after a pronoun is *'d*: I'*d* like to cash a check.
Why don't you fill out another form? **Why don't we** walk to the supermarket?	Use *why don't you . . . ?* and *why don't we . . . ?* to offer suggestions.
May / **Can** I help you?	Salespeople often use these questions to offer help to a customer.

EXERCISE 37 Read the following conversation between a salesperson (S) and a customer (C) in an electronics store. Change the underlined words to make the conversation more polite. Change the punctuation if necessary. Answers may vary.

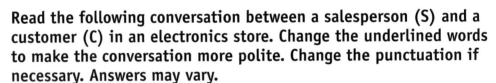

          May I help you?

S: <u>What do you need</u>?
     (example)

C: <u>I want</u> to buy a new computer. <u>Show</u> me your latest models.
     (1)   *(2)*

S: <u>Do you want</u> to see the laptops or the desktops?
     (3)

C: <u>Show</u> me the desktops.
     (4)

S: This is one of our most popular desktops.

C: <u>Turn</u> it on.
     (5)

S: It *is* on. Just hit the space bar.

C: I don't know how much memory to buy.

S: How do you use your computer?

C: We like to play games and watch movies.

S: Then <u>buy</u> this computer, which has a lot of memory and speed.
(6)

C: <u>Tell</u> me the price.
(7)

S: We have a great deal on this one. It's $1,299. If you buy it this week, you can get a $200 rebate from the manufacturer.

C: <u>Let me take</u> it home and try it out.
(8)

S: No problem. If you're not happy with it, you can return it within 30 days and get your money back. <u>Do you want</u> to buy a service contract?
(9)

C: What's that?

S: If you have any problem with the computer for the next two years, we will replace it for free. The contract costs $129.99.

C: <u>Let me see</u> the service contract.
(10)

S: Here's a copy. Take this card to the customer service desk and someone will bring you your computer.

C: Thanks.

S: Have a nice day.

C: You too.

Summary of Lesson 9

1. **Imperatives**

   Sit down. **Don't** be late.

2. *Let's*

   Let's go to the movies. **Let's not** be late.

3. Infinitive Patterns

   He wants **to go**.
   It's necessary **to learn** English.
   I'm afraid **to stay**.
   I use coupons **to save** money.
   I want them **to help** me.

4. Modals

MODAL	EXAMPLES	EXPLANATION
can can't	He **can** speak English. An 18-year-old **can** vote. **Can** I borrow your pen? You **can't** park here. It's a bus stop. I **can't** help you now. I'm busy.	He has this ability. He has permission. I'm asking permission. It is not permitted. I am not able to.
should shouldn't	You **should** eat healthy food. You **shouldn't** drive if you're sleepy.	It's good advice. It's a bad idea.
may may not	**May** I borrow your pen? I **may** buy a new car. I **may not** be here tomorrow.	I'm asking permission. This is possible. This is possible.
might might not	It **might** rain tomorrow. We **might not** have our picnic.	This is possible. This is possible.
must must not	A driver **must** have a license. I'm late. I **must** hurry. You **must not** drive without a license.	This is a legal necessity. This is a personal necessity. This is against the law.
will will not	The manufacturer **will** send you a check. You **will not** receive the check right away.	This is in the future.
would would like	**Would** you help me move? I **would like** to use your pen.	I'm asking a favor. I want to use your pen.
could	**Could** you help me move?	I'm asking a favor.
have to not have to	She **has to** leave. She **doesn't have to** stay.	It's necessary. It's not necessary.

Editing Advice

1. Don't use *to* after a modal.

    I must ~~to~~ go.

2. Use *to* between verbs.

    They like ^to^ play.

3. Always use the base form after a modal.

    He can swims.

    She can't ~~driving~~ *drive* the car.

4. Use the base form in an infinitive.

    He wants to goes.

    I wanted to worked.

5. We can introduce an infinitive with *it* + an adjective.

    ~~Is~~ *It's* important to get exercise.

6. Use the correct word order in a question.

    Why ~~you can't~~ *can't you* stay?

7. Use an infinitive after some adjectives.

    I'm happy ^to^ meet you.

    It's necessary ^to^ have a job.

8. Use *to*, not *for*, to show purpose.

    We went to the theater ~~for~~ *to* see a play.

9. Use the object pronoun and an infinitive after *want, expect, need*, etc.

    I want ~~he closes~~ *him to close* the door.

Editing Quiz

Some of the shaded words and phrases have mistakes. Find the mistakes and correct them. If the shaded words are correct, write *C*.

To: lovetodrive2@e*mail.com
Subject: Buying a GPS

Dear Son,

C   *get*
Recently I bought a flat-screen TV and I wanted to ~~got~~ the best price. Now
       (example)   (example)

you say that you want I help you choose a new GPS.
                            (1)

I want you be a good shopper. First, do the research. Is important compare
   (2)   (3)

prices at different stores, so buy the Sunday newspaper for look at ads.
                                             (4)

You can to look for prices online too. Remember that if you buy online,
      (5)

you have pay for shipping too. Go to the stores and try use the product. It
   (6)   (7)

might look good online, but you need to see it and try it out.
  (8)   (9)

It's not always easy make a decision. But if you follow this advice, you
                  (10)

can be a smart shopper. Let me know if you need help with something else.
  (11)

I'm always happy help you. And dear, when you can help me move some
          (12)   (13)

furniture? I sometimes need you to help me too!
                    (14)

Love, Mom

Lesson 9 Test/Review

PART 1   **Fill in the first blanks with _to_ or nothing (X). Then write the negative form in the second blank.**

EXAMPLES   I'm ready ____to____ study Lesson 10.

I _'m not ready to study_ Lesson 11.

You should ____X____ drive carefully.

You ____shouldn't drive____ fast.

1. I need _____ learn English. I _____ Polish.

2. You must _____ stop at a red light. You _____ on the highway.

3. The teacher expects _____ pass most of the students. She _____ all of the students.

4. We want _____ study grammar. We _____ literature.

5. The teacher has _____ give grades. He _____ an A to everyone.

6. We might _____ have time for some questions later. We _____ time for a discussion.

7. It's important _____ practice American pronunciation now. It _____ British pronunciation.

8. It's easy _____ learn one's native language. It _____ a foreign language.

9. Let's _____ speak English in class. _____ our native languages in class.

10. You must attend the meeting. Please _____ be here at six o'clock. _____ late.

PART 2   **Change each sentence to a question.**

EXAMPLES   I'm afraid to drive.

Why _____ *are you afraid to drive?* _____

He can help you.

When _____ *can he help me?* _____

1. You should wear a seat belt.

   Why _____

2. I want to buy some grapes.

   Why _____

3. He must fill out the application.

   When _____

4. She needs to drive to New York.

   When _____

5. You can't park at a bus stop.

   Why _____

6. It's necessary to eat vegetables.

   Why _____

7. She has to buy a car.

   Why _____

8. They'd like to see you.

   When _____

PART 3   **This is a phone conversation between a woman (W) and her mechanic (M). Choose the correct words to fill in the blanks.**

W: This is Cindy Fine. I'm calling about my car.

M: I _____ *can't* _____ hear you. _____
       (example: can't / may not)   (1 could / might)

   you speak louder, please?

W: This is Cindy Fine. Is my car ready yet?

M: We're working on it now. We're almost finished.

W: When _____ I pick it up?
       (2 would / can)

M: It will be ready by four o'clock.

W: How much will it cost?

M: $375.

W: I don't have that much money right now. _____
(3 Can / Might)

I pay by credit card?

M: Yes. You _____ use any major credit card.
(4 may / might)

Later, at the mechanic's shop:

M: Your car's ready, ma'am. The engine problem is fixed. But you

_____ replace your brakes. They're not so good.
(5 may / should)

W: _____ do it right away?
(6 Do I have to / May I)

M: No, you _____ do it immediately, but you
(7 must not / don't have to)

_____ do it within a month or two. If you don't do
(8 would / should)

it soon, you _____ have an accident.
(9 may / would)

W: How much will it cost to replace the brakes?

M: It _____ cost about $200.
(10 would / will)

W: I _____ like to make an appointment to take care
(11 will / would)

of the brakes next week. _____ I bring my car in
(12 Can / Will)

next Monday?

M: Yes, Monday is fine. You _____ bring it in early
(13 could / should)

because we get very busy later in the day.

W: OK. See you Monday morning.

PART 4 **Decide if the sentences have the same meaning or different meanings. Write _S_ for same, _D_ for different.**

EXAMPLES   Would you like to go to a movie? Do you want to go to a movie?   S

We will not go to New York. We should not go to New York.   D

1. You should go to the doctor. You can go to the doctor.

2. I may buy a new car. I must buy a new car.

3. Could you help me later? Would you help me later?

4. She must not drive her car. She doesn't have to drive her car.

5. She has to leave immediately. She must leave immediately.

6. We will have a test soon. We may have a test soon.

7. I can't go to the party. I might not go to the party.

8. You shouldn't buy a car. You don't have to buy a car.

9. May I use your phone? Could I use your phone?

10. He might not eat lunch. He may not eat lunch.

11. I should go to the doctor. I must go to the doctor.

12. I have to take my passport with me. I should take my passport with me.

PART 5 **Circle the correct word(s) to complete each sentence.**

1. If you sample a product in a supermarket, you (_don't have to / shouldn't_) buy it.

2. If you have just a few items, you (_shouldn't / don't have to_) use a shopping cart. You (_can / must_) use a small basket.

3. You (_must / should_) use coupons to save money.

4. You (_shouldn't / don't have to_) pay with cash. You can use a credit card.

5. Salesperson to customer: (_May / Would_) I help you?

6. You (_must / should_) make a list before going shopping.

7. You (_don't have to / must not_) take your own bags to the supermarket. Bags are free.

8. Try this new pizza. You (_should / might_) like it.

9. You (_can't / shouldn't_) use coupons after the expiration date.

10. You (_must not / don't have to_) park in a handicapped parking space. It's against the law.

Expansion

1 Imagine that a friend of yours is getting married. You are giving him or her advice about marriage. Write some advice for this person. You may work with a partner or compare your advice to your partner's advice when you are finished.

It's important	It's not important
It's important to be honest.	It's not important to do everything together.

2 Imagine that a friend of yours is going to travel to the U.S. You are giving him or her advice about the trip and life in the U.S. Write as many things as you can in each box. Then find a partner and compare your advice to your partner's advice.

It's necessary OR It's important OR You should	It's difficult OR You shouldn't
It's necessary to have a passport.	It's difficult to understand American English.

3 Working in a small group, write a list to give information to a new student or to a foreign student. If you need more space, use your notebook.

should or shouldn't	You should bring your transcripts to this college.
must or have to	
don't have to	
might or might not	
can or can't	

4 With a partner, write a few instructions for one of the following situations.

EXAMPLE   using a microwave oven
You shouldn't put anything metal in the microwave.
You can set the power level.
You should rotate the dish in the microwave. If you don't, the food might not cook evenly.

    a. preparing for the TOEFL®6

    b. taking a test in this class

    c. preparing for the driver's test in this state

6The *TOEFL*® is the Test of English as a Foreign Language.

⑤ Bring in an application. (Bring two of the same application, if possible.) It can be an application for a job, driver's license, license plate, apartment rental, address change, check-cashing card, rebate, etc. Work with a partner. One person will give instructions. The other person will fill it out.

⑥ Bring in ads from different stores. You can bring in ads from supermarkets or any other store. See what is on sale this week. Find a partner and discuss the products and the prices. Compare prices at two different stores, if possible. What do these products usually cost in your native country? Do you have all of these products in your native country?

Talk
About It

❶ Talk about ways you can save money when you shop.

❷ Do you prefer to shop alone or with a friend or relative? Explain why.

Write
About It

❶ Write about the differences between shopping in the U.S. and in another country.

❷ Imagine that a new classmate just arrived from another country. Write a composition giving advice about shopping in the U.S.

> ### Shopping Advice
>
> I recently bought a flat-screen TV in the U.S.
> and would like to give advice about how to shop for
> electronics here. The Sunday newspaper often has
> flyers with the sale items for the week. You can
> compare prices before you go to the store . . .

 For more practice using grammar in context, please visit our Web site.

Grammar
Count and Noncount Nouns

Quantity Words

Context
Nutrition and Health

Nouns can be divided into two groups: count and noncount nouns.

EXAMPLES	EXPLANATION
I eat four **eggs** a week. I eat one **apple** a day. Do you like **grapes**?	Count nouns have a singular and plural form. egg—eggs grape—grapes apple—apples
I like **milk**. I drink **coffee** every day. Do you like **cheese**?	Noncount nouns have no plural form.

A Healthy Diet

Before
You Read

1. What kind of food do you like to eat? What kind of food do you dislike?

2. What are some popular dishes from your country or native culture?

CD 2, TR 13

Read the following magazine article. Pay special attention to count and noncount nouns.

It is important to eat well to maintain good **health**.

A healthy **diet** consists of a **variety** of **foods**.

You need **carbohydrates**. The best carbohydrates come from whole **grain bread**, **cereal**, and **pasta**. Brown **rice** is much healthier than white rice. **Sugar** is a carbohydrate too, but it has no real nutritional value.

Of course, you need **fruits** and **vegetables** too. But not all vegetables are equally good. **Potatoes** can raise the sugar in your **blood**, which can be a **problem** for people with diabetes. It is better to eat **carrots**, **broccoli**, **corn**, and **peas**.

You also need **protein**. Red **meat** is high in protein, but a diet with a lot of red meat can cause heart disease, diabetes, and cancer. Better **sources** of protein are **chicken**, **fish**, **beans**, **eggs**, and **nuts**. Some people worry that eggs contain too much **cholesterol**. (Cholesterol is a **substance** found in animal foods.) But recent studies show that eating one egg a **day** is not usually harmful and gives us other nutritional **benefits**.

Did You
Know?

Americans spend $23.7 billion on vitamin and mineral supplements a year.

Many **people** think that all **fat** is bad. But this is not true. The fat in **nuts** (especially **walnuts**) and olive **oil** is very healthy. The fat in **butter** and **cheese** is not good.

It is not clear how much **milk** and other dairy **products** an **adult** needs. It is true that dairy products are a good source of **calcium**, but a calcium supplement can give you what you need without the fat and **calories** of milk.

The best way to stay healthy is to eat the right kinds of **food**. Food **packages** have information about **nutrition** and **calories**. You should read the package to avoid artificial **ingredients** and high levels of fat and sugar. It is also important to control your **weight** and to exercise every day.

10.2 Noncount Nouns

Noncount nouns fall into four different groups.

Group A: Nouns that have no distinct, separate parts. We look at the whole.

milk	air	meat
oil	pork	butter
water	cholesterol	poultry
coffee	paper	cheese
tea	soup	
yogurt	bread	

Group B: Nouns that have parts that are too small or insignificant to count.

rice	snow	hair
sugar	sand	grass
salt	corn	popcorn

Group C: Nouns that are classes or categories of things. The members of the category are not the same.

money (nickels, dimes, dollars)
food (vegetables, meat, spaghetti)
candy (chocolates, mints, candy bars)
furniture (chairs, tables, beds)
clothing (sweaters, pants, dresses)
mail (letters, packages, postcards)
fruit (cherries, apples, grapes)
makeup (lipstick, blush, eye shadow)
homework (compositions, exercises, reading)

(continued)

Group D: Nouns that are abstractions.

love	advice	happiness
life	knowledge	education
time	nutrition	experience
truth	intelligence	crime
beauty	unemployment	music
luck	patience	art
fun	noise	work
help	information	health

EXERCISE 1 Fill in the blanks with a noncount noun. Answers will vary.

EXAMPLE   Brown _____ *rice* _____ is healthier than

white _____ *rice* _____.

1. Babies need to drink a lot of _____, but adults don't.

2. Food from animals contains _____.

3. Children like to eat _____, but it's not good for
   their teeth.

4. Food packages have information about _____.

5. Some people put _____ in their coffee.

6. _____ is a good source of fat. _____
   is not a good source of fat.

7. _____ contains caffeine. Don't drink it at night.

8. People with high blood pressure shouldn't put a lot of
   _____ on their food.

9. Soda and candy contain a lot of _____.

EXERCISE **2** **Fill in the blanks with a noncount noun from the lists on pages 307–308. Answers may vary.**

EXAMPLE Students at registration need _____information_____ .

1. I get a lot of _____ every day in my mailbox.

2. In the winter, there is a lot of _____ in the northern parts of the U.S.

3. In the U.S., people eat _____ in a movie theater.

4. Students have to do _____ every day.

5. When you walk on the beach, you get _____ in your shoes.

6. Money doesn't buy _____ .

7. Our parents often give us a lot of _____ about how to live our lives.

8. Some cities have a lot of _____ . Many people are without jobs.

10.3 Count and Noncount Nouns

EXAMPLES	EXPLANATION

I eat a lot of **rice** and **beans**.
    rice = noncount noun
    beans = count noun
	Count and noncount are grammatical terms, but they are not always logical. *Rice* is very small and is a noncount noun. *Beans* and *peas* are also very small, but they are count nouns.

a. He eats a lot of **fruit**. a. She bought a lot of **food** for the party. b. Oranges and lemons are **fruits** that contain vitamin C. b. **Foods** that contain a lot of cholesterol are not good for you.	a. Use *fruit* and *food* as noncount nouns when you mean fruit and food in general. b. Use *fruits* and *foods* as count nouns when you mean kinds of fruit or categories of food.
a. **Candy** is not good for your health. b. There are three **candies** on the table.	a. When you talk about candy in general, *candy* is noncount. b. When you consider individual pieces of candy, you can use the plural form.

Language Note:
Other words that have both a count and a noncount form are: *time, experience, life, trouble, noise, pie*.

Fill in the blanks with the singular or plural form of the word in parentheses ( ). Use the singular for noncount nouns. Use the plural for count nouns.

EXAMPLE Add ___*peas*___ to the soup. Then put in some ___*salt*___.
(pea)   (salt)

1. Do you like to eat _____?
(fruit)

2. Oranges, grapefruits, and lemons are _____ that have a lot
(fruit)
of vitamin C.

3. When children eat a lot of _____, they sometimes get sick.
(candy)

4. Let's go shopping. There is no _____ in the house.
(food)

5. Milk and eggs are _____ that contain cholesterol.
(food)

6. She's going to make _____ and _____ for dinner.
(rice)   (bean)

10.4 Describing Quantities of Count and Noncount Nouns

EXAMPLES	EXPLANATION
She ate three **apples** today. He ate four **eggs** this week.	We can put a number before a count noun.
I ate two **slices of bread**. Please buy a **bottle of olive oil**. She drank three **glasses of milk**.	We cannot put a number before a noncount noun. We use a unit of measure, which we can count.

Ways we see noncount nouns:

BY CONTAINER	BY PORTION	BY MEASUREMENT[1]	BY SHAPE OR WHOLE PIECE	OTHER
a bottle of water a carton of milk a jar of pickles a bag of flour a can of soda (pop)[2] a bowl of soup a cup of coffee a glass of milk	a slice (piece) of bread a piece of meat a piece of cake a piece (sheet) of paper a slice of pizza a piece of candy a strip of bacon	a spoonful of sugar a scoop of ice cream a quart of oil a pound of meat a gallon of gasoline	a loaf of bread an ear of corn a piece of fruit a head of lettuce a candy bar a tube of toothpaste a bar of soap	a piece of mail a piece of furniture a piece of advice a piece of information a work of art

[1]For a list of conversions from the American system of measurement to the metric system, see Appendix G.
[2]Some Americans say "soda"; others say "pop."

EXERCISE 4 Fill in the blanks with a logical quantity for each of these noncount nouns. Answers may vary.

EXAMPLES   She bought _____*one pound of*_____ coffee.

She drank _____*two cups of*_____ coffee.

1. She ate _____ meat.

2. She bought _____ meat.

3. She bought _____ bread.

4. She ate _____ bread.

5. She bought _____ rice.

6. She ate _____ rice.

7. She bought _____ sugar.

8. She put _____ sugar in her coffee.

9. She ate _____ soup.

10. She ate _____ corn.

11. She bought _____ gas for her car.

12. She put _____ motor oil into her car's engine.

13. She used _____ paper to do her homework.

10.5 *A Lot Of, Much, Many*

Use *many* for count nouns. Use *much* for noncount nouns. Use *a lot of* for both count and noncount nouns.

	COUNT (PLURAL)	NONCOUNT
Affirmative	He baked **many** cookies. He baked **a lot of** cookies.	He baked **a lot of** bread.
Negative	He didn't bake **many** cookies. He didn't bake a **lot of** cookies.	He didn't bake **much** bread. He didn't bake **a lot of** bread.
Question	Did he bake **many** cookies? Did he bake **a lot of** cookies? **How many** cookies did he bake?	Did he bake **much** bread? Did he bake **a lot of** bread? **How much** bread did he bake?

Language Notes:
1. *Much* is rarely used in affirmative statements. Use *a lot of* in affirmative statements.
2. When the noun is omitted (in the following case, *cookies*), use *a lot*, not *a lot of*.
   He baked a lot of cookies, but he didn't eat **a lot**.

EXERCISE 5   Fill in the blanks with *much*, *many*, or *a lot of*. In some cases, more than one answer is possible.

EXAMPLES   She doesn't eat ____much____ pasta.

____Many____ American supermarkets are open 24 hours a day.

__A lot of__ sugar is not good for you.

1. In the summer in the U.S., there's _____ corn.

2. Children usually drink _____ milk.

3. _____ people have an unhealthy diet.

4. I drink coffee only about once a week. I don't drink _____ coffee.

5. There are _____ places that sell fast food.

6. It's important to drink _____ water.

7. How _____ glasses of water did you drink today?

8. How _____ fruit did you eat today?

9. How _____ cholesterol is there in one egg?

10. It isn't good to eat _____ candy.

11. We should eat _____ vegetables.

10.6 A Few, A Little

	EXAMPLES	EXPLANATION
Count	I bought **a few** bananas. She ate **several** cookies. She drank **a few** cups of tea.	Use *a few* and *several* with count nouns or with quantities that describe noncount nouns (*cup, bowl, piece*, etc.).
Noncount	He ate **a little** meat. He drank **a little** tea.	Use *a little* with noncount nouns.

EXERCISE 6   Fill in the blanks with *a few*, *several*, or *a little*.

EXAMPLES   He has ___a few___ good friends.

He has ___a little___ time to help you.

1. Every day we study _____ grammar.

2. We do _____ exercises in class.

3. The teacher gives _____ homework every day.

4. We do _____ pages in the book each day.

5. _____ students always get an A on the tests.

6. It's important to eat _____ fruit every day.

7. It's important to eat _____ pieces of fruit every day.

8. I use _____ milk in my coffee.

9. I receive _____ mail every day.

10. I receive _____ letters every day.

10.7 *Some, Any, No,* and *A/An*

	SINGULAR COUNT	PLURAL COUNT	NONCOUNT
Affirmative	I ate **a** peach. I ate **an** apple.	I ate **some** peaches. I ate **some** apples.	I ate **some** bread.
Question	Do you want **a** sandwich?	Do you want **any** fries? Do you need **some** napkins?	Do you want **any** salt? Do you need **some** ketchup?
Negative	I don't need **a** fork.	There aren't **any** potatoes in the soup. There are **no** potatoes in the soup.	There isn't **any** salt in the soup. There is **no** salt in the soup.

Language Notes:
1. We can use *any* or *some* for questions with plural or noncount nouns.
2. Use *any* after a negative verb. Use *no* after an affirmative verb.
   Wrong: I didn't eat *no* cherries.

EXERCISE 7 Fill in the blanks with *a, an, some,* or *any*. In some cases, more than one answer is possible.

EXAMPLE I ate ____*an*____ apple.

1. I ate _____ corn.

2. I didn't buy _____ potatoes.

3. Did you eat _____ watermelon?

4. I don't have _____ sugar.

5. There are _____ apples in the refrigerator.

6. There aren't _____ oranges in the refrigerator.

7. Do you want _____ orange?

8. Do you want _____ cherries?

9. I ate _____ banana.

10. I didn't eat _____ strawberries.

EXERCISE 8 **Make a statement about people in this class with the words given and an expression of quantity. Practice count nouns.**

EXAMPLES Vietnamese student(s)
There are a few Vietnamese students in this class.

Cuban student(s)
There's one Cuban student in this class.

1. Polish student(s)
2. Spanish-speaking student(s)
3. American(s)
4. child(ren)
5. woman/women

6. man/men
7. teacher(s)
8. American citizen(s)
9. senior citizen(s)
10. teenager(s)

EXERCISE 9 **Fill in the blanks with an appropriate expression of quantity. In some cases, more than one answer is possible. Practice noncount nouns.**

EXAMPLE Eggs have ___a lot of___ cholesterol.

1. You shouldn't eat so much red meat because meat has _____ fat.
2. Only animal products contain cholesterol. There is _____ cholesterol in fruit.
3. Diet colas use a sugar substitute. They don't have _____ sugar.
4. There is _____ sugar in a cracker, but not much.
5. Plain popcorn is healthy, but buttered popcorn has _____ fat.
6. Coffee has caffeine. Tea has _____ caffeine too, but not as much as coffee.
7. She doesn't drink _____ tea. She drinks tea only occasionally.
8. I usually put _____ butter on a slice of bread.
9. I'm going to put some sugar in my coffee. Do you want _____ sugar in your coffee?
10. My sister is a vegetarian. She doesn't eat _____ meat at all. She doesn't eat _____ fish or chicken either.

EXERCISE 10 **ABOUT YOU** **Ask a question with *much* and the words given. Use *eat* or *drink*. Another student will answer. Practice noncount nouns.**

EXAMPLES candy

A: Do you eat much candy?
B: No. I don't eat any candy.

orange juice

A: Do you drink much orange juice?
B: Yes. I drink a lot of orange juice.

Eat	Drink
1. rice	7. apple juice
2. fish	8. lemonade
3. chicken	9. milk
4. pork	10. tea
5. bread	11. coffee
6. cheese	12. soda or pop

EXERCISE 11 **ABOUT YOU** Ask a question with "Do you have . . ." and the words given. Another student will answer. Practice both count and noncount nouns.

EXAMPLES   American friends

A: Do you have any American friends?
B: Yes. I have a lot of American friends.

free time

A: Do you have any free time?
B: No. I don't have any free time.

1. money with you now
2. credit cards
3. bread at home
4. bananas at home
5. orange juice in your refrigerator
6. plants in your home
7. family pictures in your wallet
8. time to relax

EXERCISE 12 This is a conversation between a husband (H) and wife (W). Choose the correct word(s) to fill in the blanks.

CD 2, TR 14

H: Where were you today? I called you from work

___**many**___ times, but there was no answer.
(examples: much / many)

W: I went to the supermarket today. I bought

_____ things.
(1 a little / a few)

H: What did you buy?

W: There was a special on coffee, so I bought _____ coffee.
(2 a lot of / much)

I didn't buy _____ fruit because the prices were very high.
(3 any / no)

H: How _____ money did you spend?
(4 much / many)

W: I spent _____ money because of the coffee. I bought 10
(5 much / a lot of)

one-pound bags.

(continued)

H: It took you a long time.

W: Yes. The store was very crowded. There were _____ people
(6 much / many)

in the store. And there was _____ traffic at that hour,
(7 a lot of / much)

so it took me _____ time to drive home.
(8 a lot of / much)

H: There's not _____ time to cook.
(9 much / many)

W: Maybe you can cook today and let me rest?

H: Uh . . . I don't have _____ experience. You do it better.
(10 much / no)

You have _____ experience.
(11 a lot of / much)

W: Yes. I have _____ because I do it all the time!
(12 a lot of / a lot)

EXERCISE 13 This is a conversation between a waitress (W) and a customer (C). Fill in the blanks with an appropriate quantity word. In some cases, more than one answer is possible.

CD 2, TR 15

W: Would you like ___*any* OR *some*___ coffee, sir?
(example)

C: Yes, and please bring me _____ cream too. I don't
(1)

need _____ sugar. And I'd like a _____ of orange juice too.
(2)   (3)

A few minutes later:

W: Are you ready to order, sir?

C: Yes. I'd like the scrambled eggs with three _____ of bacon. And some
(4)

pancakes too.

W: Do you want _____ syrup with your pancakes?
(5)

C: Yes. What kind do you have?

W: We have _____ different kinds: strawberry, cherry, blueberry,
(6)

maple . . .

C: I'll have the strawberry syrup. And bring me _____ butter too.
(7)

After the customer is finished eating:

W: Would you like _____ dessert?
(8)

C: Yes. I'd like a _____ cherry pie. And put _____ ice cream on
(9)   (10)

the pie. And I'd like _____ more coffee, please.
(11)

After the customer eats dessert:

W: Would you like anything else?

C: Just the check. I don't have _____ cash with me. Can I pay by
(12)
credit card?

W: Of course.

Eat Less, Live Longer

Before You Read

1. Do you think the American diet is healthy?
2. Do you see a lot of overweight Americans?

CD 2, TR 16

**Read the following magazine article. Pay special attention to
too much, *too many*, and *a lot of*.**

About 66% of Americans are overweight. The typical American consumes **too many** calories and **too much** fat and doesn't get enough exercise. Many American children are overweight too. Children spend **too much** time in front of the TV and not enough time getting exercise. Fifty percent of commercials shown during children's programs are for food products. Children see as many as 21 commercials advertising food per day.

Fifty percent of American pets are overweight too. Like their owners, they eat **too much** and don't get enough exercise.

There is evidence that eating fewer calories can help us live longer. Doctors studied the people on the Japanese island of Okinawa, who eat 40% less than the typical American. The Okinawan diet is low in calories and salt. Also Okinawans eat **a lot of** fruit, vegetables, and fish and drink **a lot of** green tea and water. Okinawa has **a lot of** people over the age of 100.

How can we live longer and healthier lives? The answer is simple: eat less and exercise more.

10.8 *A Lot Of* vs. *Too Much/Too Many*

EXAMPLES	EXPLANATION
It is good to eat **a lot of** fruit. In Okinawa, there are **a lot of** people over the age of 100. I don't eat **a lot** in the morning.	*A lot (of)* shows a large quantity. It is a neutral term.
You shouldn't eat a lot of ice cream because it has **too many** calories. If you drink **too much** coffee, you won't sleep tonight.	*Too much* and *too many* show that a quantity is excessive and causes a problem. Use *too many* with count nouns. Use *too much* with noncount nouns.
If you eat **too much**, you will gain weight.	Use *too much* after verbs.

EXERCISE **14** **Circle the correct words to fill in this conversation between a mother (M) and her 12-year-old son (S).**

CD 2, TR 17

M: I'm worried about you. You spend too (*much* / (*many*)) hours in front
(example)
of the TV. And you eat too (*much* / *many*) junk food and don't get
(1)
enough exercise. You're getting fat.

S: Mom. I know I watch (*a lot of* / *a lot*) TV, but I learn (*a lot* / *a lot of*)
(2) *(3)*
from TV.

M: No, you don't. Sometimes you have (*a lot of / too much*) homework,
      (4)
      but you turn on the TV as soon as you get home from school.
      I'm going to make a rule: no TV until you finish your homework.

S: Oh, Mom. You have too (*much / many*) rules.
      (5)

M: That's what parents are for: to guide their kids to make the right decisions.
      There are (*a lot of / too many*) things to do besides watching TV. Why
      (6)
      don't you go outside and play? When I was your age, we played outside.

S: "*When I was your age.*" Not again. You always say that.

M: Well, it's true. We had (*too much / a lot of*) fun outside, playing with
      (7)
      friends. I didn't have (*a lot of / too much*) toys when I was your age.
      (8)
      And I certainly didn't have video games or computer games. Also we
      helped our parents (*a lot / too much*) after school. We cut the grass
      (9)
      and washed the dishes.

S: My friend Josh cuts the grass, throws out the garbage, and cleans the
      basement once a month. His mom pays him (*too much / a lot of*)
      (10)
      money for doing it. Maybe if you pay me, I'll do it.

M: Not again. "*Josh does it. Josh has it. Why can't I?*" You always say that.
      You're not Josh, and I'm not Josh's mother. I'm not going to pay you
      for things you should do.

S: OK. Just tell me what to do, and I'll do it.

M: There are (*a lot of / too much*) leaves on the front lawn. Why don't
      (11)
      you start by putting them in garbage bags? And you can walk
      Sparky. He's getting fat too. He eats (*too much / too many*) and
      (12)
      sleeps all day. Both of you need more exercise.

EXERCISE 15   **ABOUT YOU** Fill in the blanks with *much* or *many*, and complete
                   each statement.

EXAMPLE   If I drink too ____much____ coffee, ____I won't be able to sleep tonight.____

          1. If the teacher gives too _____ homework, _____

          _____

2. If I take too _____ classes, _____

_____

3. If I eat too _____ candy, _____

_____

4. If I'm absent too _____ days, _____

_____

10.9 *Too Much/Too Many* vs. *Too*

EXAMPLES	EXPLANATION
I don't eat ice cream because it's **too** fattening. He needs to eat more. He's **too** thin.	Use *too* with adjectives and adverbs.
I don't eat ice cream because it has **too many** calories and **too much** fat.	Use *too much* and *too many* before nouns.

EXERCISE 16 **Fill in the blanks with *too*, *too much*, or *too many*.**

Situation A. Some students are complaining about the school cafeteria. They are giving reasons why they don't want to eat there.

EXAMPLE It's _____ *too* _____ noisy.

1. The food is _____ greasy.

2. There are _____ students. I can't find a place to sit.

3. The lines are _____ long.

4. The food is _____ expensive.

5. There's _____ noise.

Situation B. Some students are complaining about their class and school.

1. The classroom is _____ small.

2. We spend _____ time reviewing old lessons.

3. We have to write _____ compositions.

4. The teacher gives _____ homework.

5. There are _____ tests.

EXERCISE 17 **ABOUT YOU** Write a few sentences to complain about something: your apartment, your roommate, this city, this college, and so on. Use *too, too much,* or *too many* in your sentences.

EXAMPLE My roommate spends too much time in the bathroom in the morning. He's too messy.[3]

_____

_____

_____

EXERCISE 18 Fill in the blanks with *too, too much,* or *too many* if a problem is presented. Use *a lot of* if no problem is presented.

EXAMPLE Strawberries are _____ too _____ expensive this week. Let's not buy them.

1. There are _____ noncount nouns in English.

2. "Rice" is a noncount noun because the parts are _____ small to count.

3. If this class is _____ hard for you, you should go to a lower level.

4. Good students spend _____ time doing their homework.

5. If you spend _____ time watching TV, you won't have time for your homework.

6. It takes _____ time to learn English, but you can do it.

7. Oranges have _____ vitamin C.

8. If you are on a diet, don't eat potato chips. They have _____ calories and _____ fat.

9. Babies drink _____ milk.

10. If you drink _____ coffee, you won't sleep.

[3]A *messy* person does not put his or her things in order.

EXERCISE 19   **A doctor (D) and patient (P) are talking. Fill in the blanks with an appropriate quantity word or unit of measurement to complete this conversation. In some cases, more than one answer is possible.**

CD 2, TR 18

D: I'm looking at your lab results and I see that your cholesterol level

is very high. Also your blood pressure is _____ *too* _____ high.
(example)

Do you use _____ salt on your food?
(1)

P: Yes, Doctor. I love salt. I eat _____ potato chips and
(2)

popcorn.

D: That's not good. You're overweight too. You need to lose 50 pounds.

What do you usually eat?

P: For breakfast I usually grab _____ coffee and a
(3)

doughnut. I don't have _____ time for lunch, so I eat
(4)

_____ cookies and drink _____
(5)   (6)

soda while I'm working. I'm so busy that I have _____
(7)

time to cook at all. So for dinner, I usually stop at a fast-food place and

get a burger and fries.

D: That's a terrible diet! How _____ exercise do you get?
(8)

P: I never exercise. I don't have _____ time at all. I own
(9)

my own business and I have _____ work. Sometimes I
(10)

work 80 hours a week.

D: I'm going to give you an important _____ advice.
(11)

You're going to have to change your lifestyle.

P: I'm _____ old to change my habits.
(12)

D: You're only 45 years old. You're _____ young to die.
(13)

And if you don't change your habits, you're going to have a heart

attack. I'm going to give you a booklet about staying healthy. It has

_____ information that will teach you about diet
(14)

and exercise. Please read it and come back in six months.

Summary of Lesson 10

Words that we use before count and noncount nouns:

WORD	COUNT (SINGULAR) EXAMPLE: *BOOK*	COUNT (PLURAL) EXAMPLE: *BOOKS*	NONCOUNT EXAMPLE: *TEA*
the	x	x	x
a	x		
one	x		
two, three, etc.		x	
some (affirmatives)		x	x
any (negatives and questions)		x	x
no	x	x	x
a lot of		x	x
much (negatives and questions)			x
many		x	
a little			x
a few		x	
several		x	

Editing Advice

1. Don't put *a* or *an* before a noncount noun.

    some
    I want to give you ~~an~~ advice.

2. Noncount nouns are always singular.

    a lot of
    My mother gave me ~~many~~ advices.

    pieces of
    He received three ˄ mails today.

3. Don't use a double negative.

    any
    He doesn't have ~~no~~ time.   OR   *He has no time.*

4. Don't use *much* with an affirmative statement.

    Uncommon: There was much rain yesterday.
    Common: There was a lot of rain yesterday.

5. Don't use *a* or *an* before a plural noun.

    She has ~~a~~ blue eyes.

6. Use the plural form for plural count nouns.

    He has a lot of friend_s.

7. Omit *of* after *a lot* when the noun is omitted.

    My English teacher gives a lot of homework. My math teacher

    gives a lot ~~of~~ too.

8. Use *of* with a unit of measure.

    I ate three pieces *of* bread.

9. Don't use *of* after *many, much, a few,* or *a little* if a noun follows directly.

    She has many ~~of~~ friends.

    He put a little ~~of~~ milk in his coffee.

10. Only use *too/too much/too many* if there is a problem.

    He has a good job. He earns ~~too much~~ *a lot of* money.

    My grandfather is ~~too~~ *very* healthy.

11. Don't use *too much* before an adjective or adverb.

    I don't want to go outside today. It's too ~~much~~ hot.

12. Don't confuse *too* and *to*.

    If you eat ~~to~~ *too* much candy, you'll get sick.

Editing Quiz

Some of the shaded words and phrases have mistakes. Find the mistakes and correct them. If the shaded words are correct, write *C*.

My parents gave me a good advice: stay healthy. They told me to get

C *(example)*

good nutrition and exercise every day. My parents follow their own advice,

(example)

and, as a result, they're too healthy. I try to follow their advices but

(1) *(2)*

sometimes I can't. I'm very busy, and sometimes I don't have no time for

(3)

exercise. When I was in high school, I had a lot of free time, but now I

don't have a lot of. So for breakfast, I just have a cup coffee with a

(4) *(5)*

little of sugar and two pieces of toasts.

(6) *(7)*

I have a lot of friend at college, and we often go out to eat after class.

(8)

But they always want to go to a fast food places. I know the food is

(9)

too much greasy. When I suggest a healthier restaurant, they say it's to

(10) *(11)*

expensive. When I get home from work at night, I just heat up a frozen

dinner. I know this is not healthy, but what can I do?

Lesson 10 Test/Review

PART 1 **Fill in the blanks with an appropriate measurement of quantity. Answers may vary.**

EXAMPLE a ___*cup*___ of coffee

1. a _____ of water
2. a _____ of sugar
3. a _____ of milk
4. a _____ of furniture
5. a _____ of soup

6. a _____ of mail
7. a _____ of advice
8. a _____ of gasoline
9. a _____ of paper
10. a _____ of toothpaste

Read the following composition. Choose the correct quantity word or indefinite article.

I had ___some___ problems when I first came to the U.S. First, I didn't
    (example: some / any / a little)

have _____ money. _____ friends of mine lent me _____
    (1 much / a / some)   (2 A few / A little / A few of)   (3 some / a / any)

money, but I didn't feel good about borrowing it.

Second, I couldn't find _____ apartment. I went to see _____
    (4 a / an / no)   (5 some / a little / an)

apartments, but I couldn't afford _____ of them. For _____
    (6 an / any / none)   (7 a little / a few of / several)

months, I had to live with my uncle's family, but the situation wasn't good.

Third, I started to study English, but soon found _____ job and
    (8 a / any / some)

didn't have _____ time to study. As a result, I was failing my course.
    (9 no / much / a few)

However, little by little my life started to improve, and I don't need

_____ help from my friends and relatives anymore.
(10 no / some / much)

Expansion

Classroom
Activities

❶ Make a list of unhealthy things that you eat. Make a list of things that you need to eat for a healthy diet.

Unhealthy things I eat	Things I should eat

2 These are some popular foods in the U.S. Put a check (✓) in the column that describes your experience of this food. Then find a partner and compare your list to your partner's list.

Food	I Like	I Don't Like	I Never Tried
pizza		✓	
hot dogs			
submarine sandwiches			
tacos			
hamburgers			
breakfast cereal			
peanut butter			
cheesecake			
tortilla chips			
potato chips			
popcorn			
chocolate chip cookies			
fried chicken			
pretzels			

3 Cross out the phrase that doesn't fit and fill in the blanks to make a true statement about the U.S. or another country. Find a partner and compare your answers.

EXAMPLE   People in _____Argentina_____ eat/~~don't eat~~ __a lot of__ meat.

a. People in _____ eat/don't eat _____ natural foods.

b. People in _____ drink/don't drink _____ tea.

c. People in _____ shop/don't shop for food every day.

d. People in _____ eat/don't eat in a movie theater.

e. People in _____ drink/don't drink _____ bottled water.

Talk About It

1 Look at the dialogue that takes place in a restaurant on pages 316–317. Do you think this man is eating a healthy breakfast? Why or why not?

2 Americans often eat some of these foods for breakfast: cereal and milk, toast and butter or jelly, orange juice, eggs, bacon, coffee. Describe a typical breakfast for you.

❸ Most American stores sell products in containers: bags, jars, cans, and so forth. How do stores in other countries sell products?

❹ Do stores in other countries give customers bags for their groceries, or do customers have to bring their own bags to the store?

❺ Some things are usually free in an American restaurant: salt, pepper, sugar, cream or milk for coffee, mustard, ketchup, napkins, water, ice, coffee refills, and sometimes bread. Are these things free in a restaurant in other countries?

❻ The following saying is about food. Discuss the meaning. Do you have a similar saying in your native language?

You are what you eat.

Write
About It

❶ Describe shopping for food in the U.S. or in another country. You may include information about the following:

- packaging
- open market vs. stores
- self-service vs. service from salespeople
- shopping carts
- fixed prices vs. negotiable prices
- freshness of food

❷ Describe food and eating habits in your native country.

Food in Mexico

In my country, Mexico, we have our main meal in the middle of the day. We eat a lot of rice and beans. We don't use much bread, like Americans do. Instead, we eat tortillas with most of our meals . . .

For more practice using grammar in context, please visit our Web site.

Grammar
Adjectives

Noun Modifiers

Adverbs

Context
Great Women

Helen Keller (1882–1968)

Helen Keller

Before
You Read

1. Do you know of any special schools for handicapped people?

2. What kinds of facilities or services does this school have for handicapped people?

CD 2, TR 19

Read the following textbook article. Pay special attention to adjectives and adverbs.

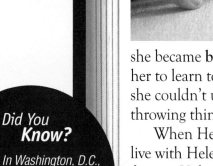

Do you know of anyone with a disability who did **remarkable** things? Helen Keller was a truly **remarkable** woman.

Helen Keller was a **healthy** baby. But when she was 19 months old, she had a **sudden** fever. The fever disappeared, but she became **blind** and **deaf**. Because she couldn't hear, it was **difficult** for her to learn to speak. As she grew, she was **angry** and **frustrated** because she couldn't understand or communicate with people. She became **wild**, throwing things and kicking and biting.

When Helen was seven years old, a teacher, Anne Sullivan, came to live with Helen's family. First, Anne taught Helen how to talk with her fingers. Helen was **excited** when she realized that things had names. Then Anne taught Helen to read by the Braille system. Helen learned these skills **quickly**. However, learning to speak was harder. Anne continued to teach Helen **patiently**. Finally, when Helen was ten years old, she could speak **clearly** enough for people to understand her.

Helen was very **intelligent**. She went to an institute for the blind, where she did very **well** in her studies. Then she went to college,[1] where she graduated with honors when she was 24 years old. Helen traveled **extensively** with Anne. She worked **tirelessly**, traveling all over America, Europe, and Asia to raise money to build schools for **blind** people. Her **main** message was that **handicapped** people are like everybody else. They want to live life **fully** and **naturally**. Helen wanted all people to be treated **equally**.

While she was in college, Helen wrote her first of many books, *The Story of My Life*, in 1903.

Did You Know?

In Washington, D.C., there is a special college for deaf students—Gallaudet University.

[1]In the U.S., the words *college* and *university* usually have the same meaning.

11.1 Adjectives and Adverbs

EXAMPLES	EXPLANATION
Helen was a **healthy** baby. She seemed **intelligent**. She became **blind**. Anne Sullivan was a **wonderful** teacher.	Adjectives describe nouns. We can use adjectives before nouns or after the verbs *be, become, look, seem,* and other sense-perception verbs.
Anne taught Helen **patiently**. Helen learned **quickly**. People want to live life **fully**.	Adverbs of manner tell how or in what way we do things. We form most adverbs of manner by putting *-ly* at the end of an adjective. Adverbs of manner usually follow the verb phrase.

EXERCISE **1** Decide if the underlined word is an adjective (*adj.*) or adverb (*adv.*).

EXAMPLES Helen was a <u>healthy</u> baby. [*adj.*]

When Helen couldn't communicate, she threw things <u>angrily</u>. [*adv.*]

1. She seemed <u>wild</u>.

2. She was <u>blind</u> and <u>deaf</u> because of a <u>serious</u> illness.

3. She had a <u>good</u> teacher.

4. She learned to speak <u>clearly</u>.

5. Anne was a <u>patient</u> woman.

6. She worked <u>tirelessly</u> with Helen.

7. Helen learned <u>enthusiastically</u>.

8. Helen wanted to live a <u>full</u> life.

9. She was a <u>remarkable</u> woman.

10. We should respect all people <u>equally</u>.

Helen Keller and Anne Sullivan

11.2 Adjectives

EXAMPLES	EXPLANATION
Anne was a **patient** teacher. Helen was an **intelligent** person.	Adjectives describe nouns.
Anne was a **good** friend. I have many **good** friends.	Adjectives are always singular. *Wrong:* I have many *goods* friends.
Helen felt **frustrated** when she couldn't communicate. She was **excited** when she learned her first word. **Handicapped** people can live a full life.	Some -ed words are adjectives: *married, divorced, excited, frustrated, handicapped, worried, finished, tired, crowded.*
Helen had an **interesting** life. She was an **amazing** woman.	Some -ing words are adjectives: *interesting, boring, amazing, exciting.*
Helen was a **normal**, **healthy** baby. Anne was a **patient**, **intelligent** teacher.	Sometimes we put two adjectives before a noun. We can separate the two adjectives with a comma.
Some people have an easy childhood. Helen had a hard **one**. Do you like serious stories or funny **ones**?	After an adjective, we can substitute a singular noun with *one* and a plural noun with *ones* to avoid repeating the noun.
Anne was **a kind teacher**. Anne was kind.	Only use an article before an adjective if a noun follows. *Wrong:* Anne was *a kind*.

EXERCISE 2   **Fill in the blanks with an appropriate adjective. (Change *a* to *an* if the adjective begins with a vowel sound.) Answers may vary.**

EXAMPLES   When Helen couldn't communicate, she became _____wild_____.

Helen was a __n interesting__ person.

1. Helen was a _____ baby.

2. Before Helen learned to communicate, she felt

   very _____.

3. She had a _____ life.

4. She wanted _____ treatment for blind people.

5. Helen had a _____ teacher.

6. Helen was a very _____ woman.

7. The story about Helen Keller was _____.

8. _____ people can read with the Braille method.

EXERCISE 3 Fill in the blanks with an appropriate adjective. (Change *a* to *an* if the adjective begins with a vowel sound.) Answers may vary.

EXAMPLES This is a _____big_____ class.

This is a __n easy__ class.

1. This classroom is _____.
2. The classrooms at this school are _____.
3. English is a _____ language.
4. This book is very _____.
5. We sometimes have _____ tests.
6. We read a _____ story about Helen Keller.
7. Did you learn any _____ words in the story?

EXERCISE 4 **ABOUT YOU** Ask a question of preference with the words given. Follow the example. Use *one* or *ones* to substitute for the noun. Another student will answer.

EXAMPLES an easy exercise/hard

A: Do you prefer an easy exercise or a hard one?
B: I prefer a hard one.

funny movies/serious

A: Do you prefer funny movies or serious ones?
B: I prefer funny ones.

1. a big city/small
2. an old house/new
3. a cold climate/warm
4. a small car/big
5. a soft mattress/hard
6. green grapes/red
7. red apples/yellow
8. strict teachers/easy
9. noisy children/quiet
10. used textbooks/new

A Special Athlete

Before
You Read

1. Do you know any disabled people who participate in sports?

2. Did you see the most recent Olympic games?

CD 2, TR 20

Read the following magazine article. Pay special attention to nouns that describe nouns.

Gina McWilliams is an inspiring person and great athlete.

As a child, she loved sports, but when she was 26 years old, she was in a **car accident** and lost part of her right leg. She still wanted to compete in sports. She tried many sports, including **waterskiing** and basketball, which she played in a **wheelchair**, before she decided on volleyball. At the 2008 Paralympic Games[2] in China, she and her team won the **silver medal**. When Gina's not practicing volleyball, she's busy raising her two children and working as a **sports director** for disabled adults and children.

[2]In the *Paralympic Games*, athletes with physical and visual disabilities compete.

11.3 Noun Modifiers

EXAMPLES	EXPLANATIONS
Gina is a **volleyball player**. Her team won a **silver medal**.	We can use a noun to describe another noun.
Gina sometimes uses a **wheelchair**. She can play **basketball**. She enjoys **waterskiing**.	Sometimes we write the two nouns as one word. The noun modifier and the noun become a compound word.
a. Gina played wheelchair **basketball**. b. Was she a **basketball** coach?	The first noun is more specific. The second noun is more general. In sentence (a), *wheelchair basketball* is a specific kind of basketball. In sentence (b), *basketball coach* is a specific kind of coach.
Does Gina have a **driver's** license? Did she have a **skiing** accident?	Sometimes the first noun ends with 's or -ing.
A chair with **wheels** is a **wheel**chair. A language that uses **signs** is **sign** language. A girl who is sixteen **years** old is a sixteen-**year**-old girl.	When two nouns come together, the first one is always singular.

Language Note:
There are many noun + noun combinations. Here are a few:

winter coat	driver's license	fingernail
cell phone	bachelor's degree	flashlight
wedding ring	master's degree	haircut
garbage can	shopping cart	daylight
summer vacation	washing machine	eyebrow
TV show	skiing accident	dishwasher
math course	running shoes	doorknob
art museum	reading glasses	drugstore
peanut butter	baking dish	earring

EXERCISE **5** **Fill in the blanks. Make sure that the noun modifier is singular.**

EXAMPLE A store that sells groceries is a _____grocery store_____.

1. A store that sells books is a _____.

2. A store that has departments is a _____.

3. A department that sells shoes is a _____.

4. Language that communicates with signs is _____.

5. Glasses for eyes are _____.

6. A pot for flowers is a _____.

7. A garden of roses is a _____.

8. A bill of five dollars is a _____.

9. A child who is six years old is a _____.

10. A vacation that lasts two weeks is a _____.

11. A brush for teeth is a _____.

12. A man who is 6 feet tall is a _____.

EXERCISE 6 **Fill in the blanks by putting the words in parentheses ( ) in the correct order. Make any other necessary changes.**

Last night I saw a ___**TV program**___ about the Paralympic Games.
                    (example: program/TV)

One of the athletes is Christina Ripp. Christina is in a

_____. But that didn't stop her from becoming a
   (1 chair/wheels)

_____. She became interested in basketball when she
   (2 player/basketball)

was just a _____. She played on her
            (3 child/ten years old)

_____ at the University of Illinois. In 2005, she got her
   (4 team/college)

_____ in _____. In 2008, she won a
   (5 degree/bachelor's)   (6 community/health)

_____ at the Paralympic Games in China.
   (7 medal/gold)

EXERCISE 7 **Fill in the blanks by putting the two nouns in the correct order. Make any other necessary changes.**

EXAMPLE A popular sport at the Paralympic Games is ___**wheelchair basketball**___.
                                                        (basketball/wheelchair)

1. Christina Ripp has a _____.
                          (college/education)

2. Gina McWilliams had a _____.
                           (accident/car)

3. Gina is a _____.
              (volleyball/player)

4. Helen Keller lost her _____ when she
                           (sight/eyes)

   was a _____.
          (19 months old /baby)

5. Helen Keller had a _____.
                        (degree/college)

EXERCISE 8 **ABOUT YOU** Ask and answer. Put the two nouns in the right order and make any other necessary changes. Ask another student the question.

EXAMPLE   Do you have a (*license/driver's*)?

   A. Do you have a driver's license?
   B. No. I don't have a driver's license yet.

   1. What's your favorite (*program/TV*)?
   2. Do you have a (*phone/cell*)?
   3. How many (*phone/calls*) do you make a day?
   4. How many (*messages/text*) do you receive a day?
   5. Are you wearing a (*ring/wedding*)?
   6. What do you usually do during your (*summer/vacation*)?
   7. Do you bring a (*bag/books*) to class?
   8. Did you buy your (*text/books*) at the school (*books/store*)?

11.4 Comparing Adverbs of Manner and Adjectives

An adverb of manner tells *how* we do something. It describes the verb (action) of the sentence. An adjective describes a noun.

ADJECTIVES	ADVERBS	EXPLANATION
Anne was a **patient** teacher. Helen was a **quick** learner. She had a **clear** voice.	She taught **patiently**. She learned **quickly**. She spoke **clearly**.	We form most adverbs of manner by putting *-ly* at the end of an adjective.
This is a **fast** car. I have a **late** class. We had a **hard** test. I have an **early** appointment.	He drives **fast**. I arrived **late**. I studied **hard**. I need to wake up **early**.	Some adjectives and adverbs have the same form.
Helen was a **good** student.	She did **well** in school.	The adverb *well* is completely different from the adjective form *good*.

Observe word order with adverbs.

EXAMPLES	EXPLANATION
Helen learned sign language **quickly**. Helen **quickly** learned sign language.	An adverb of manner usually follows the verb phrase or it can come before the verb. It cannot come between the verb and the object. *Wrong:* Helen learned *quickly* sign language.
Helen learned **very** quickly. She did **very** well in college.	You can use *very* before an adverb of manner.

EXERCISE 9   Check (✓) if the sentence is true or false.

	True	False
EXAMPLE Helen lost her hearing slowly.		✓
1. Anne taught Helen patiently.		
2. Helen learned quickly.		
3. Helen never learned to speak clearly.		
4. Helen didn't do well in college.		
5. Helen wanted deaf people to be treated differently from hearing people.		

11.5 Spelling of -ly Adverbs

ADJECTIVE ENDING	EXAMPLE	ADVERB ENDING	ADVERB
y	easy lucky happy	Change y to i and add -ly.	eas**ily** luck**ily** happ**ily**
consonant + le	simple double comfortable	Drop the e and add -y.	simpl**y** doubl**y** comfortabl**y**
ll	full	Add -y.	full**y**
e	nice free brave	Just add -ly.	nice**ly** free**ly** brave**ly**

Language Note: There is one exception for the last rule: *true—truly*.

EXERCISE 10   Write the adverb form of each adjective. Use correct spelling.

1. bad _____

2. good _____

3. lazy _____

4. true _____

5. nice _____

6. full _____

7. responsible _____

8. polite _____

9. fast _____

10. constant _____

11. terrible _____

12. beautiful _____

EXERCISE 11 **Fill in the blanks with the adverb form of the underlined adjective.**

EXAMPLE   He's a <u>careful</u> driver. He drives _____*carefully*_____.

1. She has a <u>beautiful</u> voice. She sings _____.
2. You are a <u>responsible</u> person. You always act _____.
3. You have <u>neat</u> handwriting. You write _____.
4. I'm not a <u>good</u> swimmer. I don't swim _____.
5. He is a <u>cheerful</u> person. He always smiles _____.
6. He is <u>fluent</u> in French. He speaks French _____.
7. You have a <u>polite</u> manner. You always talk to

   people _____.
8. Nurses are <u>hard</u> workers. They work _____.
9. She looks <u>sad</u>. She said goodbye _____.
10. You are a <u>patient</u> teacher. You explain the

    grammar _____.
11. My answers are <u>correct</u>. I filled in all the

    blanks _____.

EXERCISE 12   **ABOUT YOU** **Tell how you do these things.**

EXAMPLE   write a composition
           I write a composition carefully and slowly.

1. speak English
2. speak your native language
3. dance
4. walk
5. study
6. do your homework
7. drive
8. sing
9. type
10. work
11. dress for class
12. dress for a party

EXERCISE 13   Read the story of Helen Keller's teacher, Anne Sullivan. Find the mistakes with adjectives, adverbs, and noun modifiers in the underlined words. Correct them. Not all underlined words have a mistake. If the underlined words are correct, write *C*.

                                               C

When Helen was a <u>small</u> child, she was <u>a blind</u> and <u>deaf</u>. She behaved
                   (example)   (example)   (1)

<u>wild</u>. When she was a seven-<u>years</u>-old child, her parents found a <u>wonderful</u>
(2)   (3)   (4)

teacher to work with her. The teacher's name was Anne Sullivan.

Anne was from a <u>poorly</u> immigrant family. She had a <u>terrible</u> life.
                  (5)   (6)

When she was a <u>child small</u>, she had a disease that left her almost blind.
               (7)

When she was eight <u>years</u> old, her mother died. A few years later, her
                    (8)

father abandoned the family, and Anne went to live in an orphanage.

When she was 14 years old, she could not see <u>clear</u> and she could
                                      (9)

not read. But she got the opportunity to go to a school for the blind. So at

the age of 14, she started <u>school elementary</u>. She was a <u>student very bright</u>
                        (10)   (11)

and graduated from high school as the <u>top</u> student.
                               (12)

She heard about a job to teach <u>a blind</u> girl, Helen Keller. Anne went to
                           (13)

live with Helen's family. Anne worked <u>patient</u> with Helen, showing her that
                          (14)

things had names. Within one month, Helen learned <u>signs language</u>. After
                                  (15)

that, Helen learned <u>quickly</u> and wanted to study in school. Anne attended
               (16)

<u>classes college</u> with Helen, spelling out the lectures and reading to her after
(17)

class. Helen graduated from college with honors. Anne got <u>marry</u> in 1905,
                                     (18)

when Helen was 23. But it wasn't a <u>happy</u> marriage, and Anne separated
                           (19)

from her husband. She continued to help Helen for the rest of her life.

But her <u>sight eyes</u> became worse and she became completely blind. She
         (20)

died in 1936. Helen lived until 1968.

EXERCISE **Use the adjective in parentheses or change it to an adverb to fill in the blanks.**

CD 2, TR 21   I have two friends who are complete opposites. My friend Paula complains

<u>constantly</u> about everything. I always tell her that she is a _____
(example: constant)   *(1 healthy)*

person, and that is the most important thing in life. But she is never

_____. She says that everyone is _____. When she drives, she
(2 happy)   *(3 impolite)*

behaves _____ to other drivers. She says they're all _____, but I
(4 rude)   *(5 crazy)*

think Paula is the crazy one. She doesn't make changes _____. She
(6 easy)

had to move two months ago, and she hates her _____ apartment.
(7 new)

I think it's a _____ apartment, but she finds something wrong with
(8 nice)

everything.

I have another friend, Karla. Karla is handicapped, in a wheelchair,

but she has a _____ attitude about life. She's also an _____
(9 positive)   *(10 active)*

person. She swims _____. She's always learning new things. She's
(11 good)

studying French and can speak it _____ now. She learns _____
(12 fluent)   *(13 quick)*

and is _____ about everything. She goes to museums _____
(14 curious)   *(15 frequent)*

and knows a lot about art. She is a good role model for her friends.

Adjectives; Noun Modifiers; Adverbs   **341**

Grandma Moses

1. Do you know of any old people who have a healthy, good life?

2. Who is the oldest member of your family? Is he or she in good health?

CD 2, TR 22

Read the following magazine article. Pay special attention to *very* and *too*.

They say you can't teach an old dog new tricks.
But is this really true? Anna Mary Moses proved that even elderly people can start a new career or take up a new hobby.

Anna Mary Moses was born in 1860. She had a **very** hard life working as a farmer's wife in New York State. She was always interested in art, but she was **too** busy working on the farm and raising her five children to paint. In her 70s, she became **too** weak to do hard farm work. She liked to do embroidery, but as she grew older, she couldn't continue because of arthritis. It was easier for her to hold a paintbrush than a needle, so she started to paint. She painted pictures of farm life. A New York City art collector saw her paintings in a drugstore window and bought them. Today, some of her paintings are in major art museums.

embroidery

Grandma Moses

When she was 92, she wrote her autobiography. At the age of 100, she illustrated a book. She was still painting when she died at age 101. Better known as "Grandma Moses," she created 1,600 paintings.

11.6 Too vs. Very

EXAMPLES	EXPLANATION
Grandma Moses was **very** old when she wrote her autobiography. Her paintings became **very** popular.	*Very* shows a large degree. It doesn't indicate any problems.
She was **too** busy working on the farm to paint. She became **too** weak to do farm work.	*Too* shows that there is a problem. We often use an infinitive phrase after *too*.

EXERCISE 15 **Fill in the blanks with *very* or *too*.**

EXAMPLES Basketball players are ___*very*___ tall.

I'm ___*too*___ short to touch the ceiling.

1. In December, it's _____ cold to go swimming outside.
2. June is usually a _____ nice month.
3. Some elderly people are in _____ good health.
4. Some elderly people are _____ sick to take care of themselves.
5. It's _____ important to know English.
6. This textbook is _____ long to finish in three weeks.
7. The president has a _____ important job.
8. The president is _____ busy to answer all his letters.
9. Some Americans speak English _____ fast for me. I can't understand them.
10. I can speak my own language _____ well.
11. When you buy a used car, you should inspect it _____ carefully.
12. A turtle moves _____ slowly.
13. If you drive _____ slowly on the highway, you might get a ticket.
14. Gina McWilliams is a _____ good athlete.
15. When Grandma Moses had arthritis, embroidery became _____ difficult for her.

11.7 Too and Enough

	EXAMPLES	EXPLANATION
Too + Adjective/Adverb	In her 70s, Grandma Moses was **too weak** to do farm work. I'm working **too hard**. I need to relax.	Use *too* **before** adjectives and adverbs. **Be careful:** Don't use *too much* before adjectives and adverbs. *Wrong:* I'm working too *much* hard.
Adjective/Adverb + *Enough*	She was **talented enough** to get the attention of an art collector. She painted **skillfully enough** to get her pictures in art museums.	Enough means "as much as needed." Use *enough* **after** adjectives and adverbs.
Enough + Noun	When she was younger, she didn't have **enough time** to paint.	Use *enough* **before** nouns.

EXERCISE 16   **Fill in the blanks with *too* or *enough* plus the word in parentheses ( ).**

EXAMPLES   Your son is four years old. He's _____ **too young** _____ to go to first grade.
(young)

My sister is 18 years old. She's _____ **old enough** _____ to get a driver's license.
(old)

1. I can't read Shakespeare in English. It's _____ for me.
(hard)

2. My brother is 21 years old. He's _____ to get married.
(old)

3. My grandfather is 90 years old and in bad health. My family takes

care of him. He's _____ to take care of himself.
(sick)

4. I saved $5,000. I want to buy a used car. I think I have _____

_____.
(money)

5. I'd like to get a good job, but I don't have _____.
(experience)

6. She wants to move that piano, but she can't do it alone. She's not

_____.
(strong)

7. The piano is _____ for one person to move.
(heavy)

8. I sit at my desk all day, and I don't get _____.
(exercise)

EXERCISE **17** Find the mistakes with the underlined words and correct them. Not all underlined words have a mistake. If the underlined words are correct, write C.

CD 2, TR 23

We just read a story about Grandma Moses. We learned that you are never too ~~much~~ old to learn something new.
(example)

I always thought I was <u>too old</u> to learn another language,
_(1)_

but now that I'm in the U.S. I have no choice. Most of

the students in class are young and learn very <u>quick</u>.
_(2)_

But I am 58 years old, and I'm not a <u>fast</u> learner at my age. I don't catch
_(3)_

on as quickly as my younger classmates. However, most of them have a

job, so they don't have <u>enough time</u> to study. Some of them have small
_(4)_

children, so they are very <u>busily</u> and don't always have <u>enough energy</u>
_(5)_ _(6)_

to do their homework. I'm not working and my children are <u>enough old</u>
_(7)_

to take care of themselves. In fact, they're in college also. So I have

<u>enough time</u> to do all my homework. My kids are <u>proudly</u> of me for going
_(8)_ _(9)_

to college at my age. My teacher always tells me I'm doing <u>too well</u> in her
_(10)_

class. After learning English, I'm planning to get a degree in history. I am

<u>too</u> interested in this subject. It was my favorite subject when I was in high
_(11)_

school. When I finish my degree, I'll be in my 60s. It will probably be

<u>too late</u> for me to find a job in this field, but I don't care. I just have a <u>very</u>
_(12)_ _(13)_

great love of this subject. My kids think it will be <u>too much</u> hard for me
_(14)_

because history books are <u>hardly</u> to read. But I am <u>too</u> motivated, so I know
_(15)_ _(16)_

I can do it. Besides, if Grandma Moses could learn to paint in her 70s and

write a book when she was 92, I can certainly study history at my age.

Grandma Moses is a very <u>well</u> role model. Who says you can't teach an
_(17)_

old dog <u>news</u> tricks?
_(18)_

Adjectives; Noun Modifiers; Adverbs   **345**

Summary of Lesson 11

1. Adjectives and Adverbs:

ADJECTIVES	ADVERBS
She has a **beautiful** voice.	She sings **beautifully**.
She is **careful**.	She drives **carefully**.
She has a **late** class.	She arrived **late**.
She is a **good** driver.	She drives **well**.

2. Adjective Modifiers and Noun Modifiers:

ADJECTIVE MODIFIER	NOUN MODIFIER
a clean window	a store window
a new store	a shoe store
warm coats	winter coats
a new license	a driver's license

3. *Very/Too/Enough:*
He's **very** healthy.
He's **too** young to retire. He's only 55.
He's old **enough** to understand life.
He has **enough** money to take a vacation.

Editing Advice

1. Don't make adjectives plural.

Those are importants ideas.

2. Put the specific noun before the general noun.

truck driver
He is a ~~driver truck~~.

3. Some adjectives end in *-ed*. Don't omit the *-ed*.

ed
I'm finish with my project.
      ^

4. If the adjective ends in *-ed*, don't forget to include the verb *be*.

is
He married.
   ^

5. A noun modifier is always singular.

She is a letters carrier.

6. Put the adjective before the noun.

very important
He had a meeting ~~very important~~.

7. Don't use an article before an adjective if there is no noun.

Your house is ~~a~~ beautiful.

8. Don't confuse *too* and *very*. *Too* indicates a problem.

very
My father is ~~too~~ healthy.

9. Don't confuse *too much* and *too*. *Too much* is followed by a noun. *Too* is followed by an adjective or adverb.

It's too ~~much~~ hot today. Let's stay inside.

10. Put *enough* after the adjective.

old
He's enough ~~old~~ to drive.

11. Don't use *very* before a verb. *Very* is used only with adjectives and adverbs.

He ~~very~~ likes the U.S. very much. or He really likes the U.S.

12. Put the adverb at the end of the verb phrase.

late
He ~~late~~ came home.

slowly
He opened ~~slowly~~ the door.

13. Use an adverb to describe a verb. Use an adjective to describe a noun.

ly
He drives careful.

That man is very nice~~ly~~.

well
You speak English very ~~good~~.

Editing Quiz

Some of the shaded words and phrases have mistakes. Find the mistakes and correct them. If the shaded words are correct, write C.

       ~~really~~   C

I ~~very~~ admire my aunt Rose. She's very intelligent. She married and has
(example)   *(example)*   *(1)*

three grown children. When her children became enough old to take care
(2)   *(3)*

of themselves, she decided to go back to college. She wants to study

programming computer. Some people say she's too much old to start a
(4)   *(5)*

new career, but she doesn't pay any attention. She loves computers.
(6)

She works part-time at a flowers shop. She thinks it's a job very interesting.
(7)   *(8)*

She meets a lot of interestings people. She's a very nice to everyone, and
(9)   *(10)*

everyone loves her. Whenever I need advice, I can go to her. She listens

patiently and treats everyone kind.
(11)   *(12)*

Rose came to the U.S. from Guatemala when she was 18. She had five

younger sisters and brothers. Her mother died when she was young,
(13)

and she had to take care of her brothers and sisters. She took care of them

wonderfully. She didn't speak one word of English when she left Guatemala.
(14)

She learned quickly English, and now she speaks English very good.
(15)   *(16)*

She's not only my aunt; she's a good friend.
(17)

Lesson 11 Test/Review

PART 1 Fill in the blanks by putting the two words in the correct order. Make any other necessary changes. Some words are already in the correct order.

EXAMPLE Grandma Moses was a <u>n old woman</u> when she started to paint.
(woman/old)

1. She painted _____.
(pictures/beautiful/very)

2. She was not _____ to learn something new.
(old/too)

3. When Helen Keller was a _____ she
(baby/nineteen/months/old)

   became very sick.

4. Helen communicated with _____.
(language/signs)

5. Gina McWilliams was in a _____ when she was
(car/accident)

   26 years old.

6. Her _____ won the _____.
(volleyball/team)   (medal/silver)

7. She sometimes uses a _____.
(chair/wheels)

8. She played volleyball _____ to be in the Paralympic
(well/enough)

   Games.

PART 2 Sue and her brother, Don, are very different. Fill in the blanks with the correct form, adjective or adverb, of the word in parentheses ( ) to describe them.

EXAMPLE Sue is a <u>patient</u> person. Don does everything <u>impatiently</u>.
(patient)   (impatient)

1. Sue has _____ handwriting. Don writes _____. I can't
(neat)   (sloppy)

   even read what he wrote.

2. She talks _____. He talks _____.
(calm)   (fast)

3. She speaks English _____. He has a _____ time with English.
(fluent)   (hard)

4. She learns languages _____. Learning a new language is _____
(easy)   (difficult)

   for Don.

5. She types _____. He makes a lot of mistakes. He needs someone
   (accurate)

   to check his work _____.
   (careful)

6. She has a very _____ voice. He speaks _____.
   (soft) *(loud)*

7. She sings _____. He sings like a _____ chicken.
   (beautiful) *(sick)*

8. She is always very _____. He sometimes behaves _____.
   (responsible) *(childish)*

9. She saves her money _____. He buys things he doesn't need.
   (careful)

   He spends his money _____.
   (foolish)

10. She exercises _____. He's very _____ about exercising.
    (regular) *(lazy)*

Expansion

Classroom Activities

❶ **Circle the words that best describe your behaviors. Find a partner and compare your personality to your partner's personality. How many characteristics do you have in common?**

a.	I usually spend my money	carefully	foolishly
b.	I do my homework	willingly	unwillingly
c.	I write compositions	carefully	carelessly
d.	I usually walk	slowly	quickly
e.	I write	neatly	sloppily
f.	I talk	fast	calmly
g.	I write my language	well	poorly
h.	Before a test, I study	hard	a little
i.	I exercise	regularly	infrequently
j.	I play tennis	well	poorly
k.	I like to live	dangerously	carefully
l.	I make important decisions	quickly	slowly and methodically
m.	I learn languages	easily	with difficulty
n.	I learn math	easily	with difficulty
o.	I make judgments	logically	intuitively

❷ Name something.

EXAMPLE   Name some things you do well.

I speak my native language well.
I swim well.

   a. Name some things you do well.

   b. Name some things you don't do well.

   c. Name some things you do quickly.

   d. Name some things you do slowly.

   e. Name something you learned to do easily.

Talk About It

❶ In a small group or with the entire class, discuss the situation of older people in your native culture. Who takes care of them when they are too old or too sick to take care of themselves? How does your family take care of its older members?

❷ In a small group or with the entire class, discuss the situation of handicapped people in the U.S. or in another country. Are there special schools? Are there special facilities, such as parking, public washrooms, and elevators?

❸ Discuss the meaning of this quote by Grandma Moses:

"What a strange thing is memory, and hope. One looks backward, the other forward; one is of today, the other of tomorrow. Memory is history recorded in our brain. Memory is a painter. It paints pictures of the past and of the day."

❹ Aristotle said, "The sign of a great teacher is that the accomplishments of his students exceed his own." What do you think this means?

Write

About It

❶ Write about a famous woman you know about who accomplished something in spite of a handicap or age.

❷ Write about a woman whom you admire very much. You may write about a famous woman or any woman you know (family member, teacher, doctor, etc.).

My Grandmother

My grandmother is a person I admire very much. After her third child was born (my mother), my grandfather died and my grandmother had to raise her family all alone. She took a job as a housekeeper to support her children . . .

 For more practice using grammar in context, please visit our Web site.

The Willis Tower, Chicago

The Space Needle, Seattle

Grammar
Comparatives

Superlatives

Context
U.S. Geography

The Empire State Building, New York

U.S. Facts

Before You Read

1. In your opinion, what is the most interesting city? Why is it interesting?

2. What cities or regions have the best climate?

CD 2, TR 24

Read the following information. Pay special attention to comparative and superlative forms.[1]

1. In area, the United States is the third **largest** country in the world (after Russia and Canada). In population, the U.S. is also the third **largest** country in the world (after China and India).
2. The **biggest** city in the U.S. in population is New York. It has about 8 million people.
3. The **tallest** building in the U.S. is the Willis Tower, in Chicago (442 meters or 1,450 feet tall). But it is not the **tallest** building in the world. That building is in Dubai (818 meters or 2,684 feet tall).
4. New York City has the **highest** cost of living in the U.S. But the cost of living in Tokyo is much **higher** than in New York.
5. Hispanics are the **fastest** growing minority in the U.S. In 2003, Hispanics passed African-Americans as the **largest** minority.
6. Rhode Island is the **smallest** state in area (1,145 square miles or 2,700 square kilometers).
7. Alaska is the **largest** state in area. Alaska is even **larger** than Colombia, South America.
8. The **least populated** state is Wyoming. It has slightly more than half a million people.
9. California is the **most populated** state. It has about 37 million people. There are **more** people in California than in Peru.
10. Valdez, Alaska, gets the **most** snow—about 326 inches per year.
11. Phoenix, Arizona, gets the **most** sunshine. Eighty-five percent of the days are sunny.
12. Mount McKinley is the **highest** mountain in the U.S. (20,320 feet or 6,193 meters). It is in Alaska.
13. There are five great lakes in the U.S. The **biggest** is Lake Superior. The others are Lake Huron, Lake Michigan, Lake Erie, and Lake Ontario.
14. The state that is the **farthest** north is Alaska. The state that is the **farthest** south is Hawaii.

> ### Did You Know?
>
> Before 1849, the population of California was very small. In 1849, gold was found in California and about 100,000 people rushed there to try to get rich.

[1]See Appendix K for a map of the U.S.

15. The **tallest** waterfall in the U.S. is in California. But Niagara Falls, in New York and Ontario, Canada, is **more famous**. It is one of the **most popular** tourist attractions. Twelve million tourists a year visit Niagara Falls. It has the **greatest** volume of water.
16. The **most recent** state to join the U.S. is Hawaii. It joined in 1959.
17. The **oldest** state is Delaware. It became a state in 1787.

Niagara Falls

12.1 Comparatives and Superlatives—An Overview

EXAMPLES	EXPLANATION
Los Angeles is **bigger** than Chicago. There are **more** people in California than in Peru.	We use the comparative form to compare two items.
New York City is the **biggest** city in the U.S. California is the **most populated** state in the U.S.	We use the superlative form to point out the number-one item in a group of three or more.

EXERCISE 1 **Circle the correct word to complete the statement.**

EXAMPLE Chicago is (bigger / (smaller)) than Los Angeles.

1. The tallest building in the world (is / isn't) in the U.S.
2. Alaska has a (larger / smaller) population than Wyoming.
3. The U.S. is (bigger / smaller) than Russia.
4. (Alaska / California) has the largest area.
5. The fastest-growing minority is (Hispanics / African Americans).
6. There are (more / fewer) Hispanics than African Americans in the U.S.
7. The most populated state is (Alaska / California).
8. The U.S. (is / isn't) the largest country in the world in area.

12.2 Comparative and Superlative Forms of Adjectives and Adverbs

	SIMPLE	COMPARATIVE	SUPERLATIVE
One-syllable adjectives and adverbs*	tall fast	taller faster	tallest fastest
Two-syllable adjectives that end in *y*	easy happy	easier happier	easiest happiest
Other two-syllable adjectives	frequent active	more frequent more active	most frequent most active
Some two-syllable adjectives have two forms.**	simple common	simpler more simple commoner more common	simplest most simple commonest most common
Adjectives with three or more syllables	important difficult	more important more difficult	most important most difficult
-ly adverbs	quickly brightly	more quickly more brightly	most quickly most brightly
Irregular adjectives and adverbs	good/well bad/badly far little a lot	better worse farther less more	best worst farthest least most

Language Notes:

*Exceptions to one-syllable adjectives:

bored	more bored	the most bored
tired	more tired	the most tired

**Other two-syllable adjectives that have two forms:
   handsome, quiet, gentle, narrow, clever, friendly, tender, stupid

Spelling Rules for Short Adjectives and Adverbs

RULE	SIMPLE	COMPARATIVE	SUPERLATIVE
Add -er and -est to short adjectives and adverbs.	tall fast	taller faster	tallest fastest
For adjectives that end in e, add -r and -st.	nice late	nicer later	nicest latest
For adjectives that end in y, change y to i and add -er and -est.	easy happy	easier happier	easiest happiest
For words ending in consonant-vowel-consonant, double the final consonant, then add -er and -est. **Exception:** Do not double final w. new—newer—newest	big sad	bigger sadder	biggest saddest

EXERCISE **2** Give the comparative and superlative forms of the word.

EXAMPLES fat   _fatter_   _fattest_

              important   **more important**   **most important**

1. interesting
2. young
3. beautiful
4. good
5. common
6. thin
7. carefully
8. pretty
9. bad
10. famous
11. lucky
12. simple
13. high
14. delicious
15. far
16. foolishly

12.3 Superlative Adjectives

EXAMPLES	EXPLANATION

New York is **the biggest** city in the U.S. California is **the most populated** state in the U.S. China has **the largest** population in the world.	We use the superlative form to point out the number-one item of a group of three or more. Use *the* before a superlative form. We often put a prepositional phrase at the end of a superlative sentence:
	
	    in the world in my family
	    in my class in my country

Niagara Falls is **one of the most popular** tourist attraction**s** in the U.S. The Willis Tower is **one of the tallest** building**s** in the world.	We often put "one of the" before a superlative form. Then we use a plural noun.

EXERCISE **3**   **Fill in the blanks with the superlative form of the word in parentheses ( ). Include *the* before the superlative form.**

EXAMPLE   Alaska is ____the largest____ state in area.
(large)

1. _____ lake in the U.S. is Lake Superior.
   (big)

2. _____ river in the U.S. is the Missouri River.
   (long)

3. _____ mountain in the U.S. is Mount McKinley.
   (high)

4. Niagara Falls is one of _____ tourist attractions.
   (popular)

5. San Francisco is one of _____ cities in the U.S.
   (expensive)

6. San Francisco is one of _____ American cities.
   (beautiful)

7. Harvard is one of _____ universities in the U.S.
   (good)

8. The Willis Tower is _____ building in the U.S.
   (tall)

9. The economy is one of _____ problems in the U.S.
   (bad)

10. Boston is one of _____ cities in the U.S.
    (old)

EXERCISE **4** **ABOUT YOU** Talk about the number-one person in your family for each of these adjectives.

EXAMPLES interesting
My aunt Rosa is the most interesting person in my family.

tall
My brother Carlos is the tallest person in my family.

1. intelligent
2. kind
3. handsome/beautiful
4. stubborn
5. lazy
6. tall

7. serious
8. nervous
9. strong
10. funny
11. responsible
12. neat

EXERCISE **5** Write a superlative sentence about each of the following items. You may include "one of the . . ." plus a plural noun.

EXAMPLE big problem today
The economy is one of the biggest problems in the U.S. today.

OR

Unemployment is the biggest problem in my country today.

1. exciting sport

2. interesting story in this book

3. bad tragedy in the world or in the U.S.

4. important invention of the last 100 years

5. interesting city in the world

6. big problem

7. bad job

8. good job

_____

9. hard teacher at this school

_____

10. popular movie star

_____

12.4 Word Order with Superlatives

EXAMPLES	EXPLANATION
What is **the biggest** lake in the U.S.? California is **the most populated** state.	A superlative adjective comes **before** a noun.
The Willis Tower is **the tallest building** in the U.S. OR **The tallest building** in the U.S. is the Willis Tower.	When the verb _be_ connects a noun to a superlative adjective + noun, there are two possible word orders.
The Hispanic population **is growing _the most quickly_** in the U.S. The population of India **is increasing _the most rapidly_** in the world.	We put superlative adverbs **after** the verb (phrase).
It **rains _the most_** in Hawaii. It **snows _the most_** in Alaska.	We put _the most, the least, the best,_ and _the worst_ **after** a verb.
Phoenix gets **_the most_ sunshine.** Alaska has **_the least_ sunshine** in the winter.	We put _the most, the least, the fewest, the best,_ and _the worst_ **before** a noun.

EXERCISE 6 **ABOUT YOU** Name the person in your family who is the superlative in each of the following activities. Put the superlative form after the verb phrase.

EXAMPLES   cook well
My mother cooks the best in the family.

eat a lot
My brother eats the most in my family.

1. talk a lot   **4.** speak English well   **7.** speak softly

2. drive well   **5.** stay up late   **8.** eat a lot

3. walk fast   **6.** get up early   **9.** dress badly

EXERCISE 7 **ABOUT YOU** Name the person in your family who is the superlative in each of the following activities. Put the superlative form before the noun.

EXAMPLE   watch a lot of TV
My brother watches the most TV. He watches TV four hours a day.

1. spend a lot of money
2. get little mail
3. drink a lot of coffee
4. spend a lot of time in the bathroom
5. spend a lot of time on the telephone
6. have a bad temper
7. make few mistakes in English

A Tale of Two Cities[2]

Before You Read

1. Compare this city to another city.
2. Do you have any friends or relatives in American cities? Do you visit them?

San Francisco

Chicago

[2]These statistics are from 2007.

CD 2, TR 25 **Look at the following chart. Then read the sentences that follow. Pay special attention to comparative forms.**

	San Francisco	Chicago
Population	800,000	2,900,000
Average cost of home	$765,000	$286,800
Unemployment	7%	5.7%
Cost of living (100 = national average)	177	128
Average family income	$68,023	$45,505
High school graduates	84.6% of population	71.8% of population
Average temperature in July	62 degrees	74 degrees
Average temperature in January	53 degrees	26 degrees
Rainfall (inches annually)	20.3	37.4
Number of clear days (no clouds) per year	160	84
Air pollution (amount of ozone in air; U.S. average = 100)	42	79
Robberies (per 100,000 people)	514	546

- Chicago has a **larger** population **than** San Francisco.
- A house in San Francisco is **more expensive than** a house in Chicago.
- Unemployment in San Francisco is **higher than** in Chicago.
- The average family income is **more** in San Francisco **than** in Chicago, but San Francisco has a **higher** cost of living.
- San Francisco has **fewer** high school graduates **than** Chicago.
- San Francisco has a **better** climate **than** Chicago. Chicago gets **more** rain **than** San Francisco. San Francisco is **sunnier than** Chicago.
- Chicago is **warmer** in the summer.
- Chicago is **colder** in the winter.
- Chicago has **more** air pollution **than** San Francisco.
- San Francisco has **less** crime than Chicago.

12.5 Comparisons

EXAMPLES	EXPLANATION
Chicago has a **larger** population **than** San Francisco. Houses in San Francisco are **more expensive than** houses in Chicago.	We use the comparative form to compare two items. We use *than* before the second item of comparison.
Chicago is **colder than** San Francisco in the winter, but it is **warmer** in the summer.	Omit *than* if the second item of comparison is not included.
San Francisco has **less** crime than Chicago. San Francisco has **fewer** people than Chicago.	The opposite of *more* is *less* or *fewer*.
The cost of living in San Francisco is **much higher than** in Chicago. Unemployment is **a little higher** in San Francisco.	*Much* or *a little* can come before a comparative form.
Formal: You know more about American cities than **I do**. **Informal:** You know more about American cities than **me**. **Formal:** I can speak English better than **he can**. **Informal:** I can speak English better than **him**.	When a pronoun follows *than*, the correct form is the subject pronoun (*he, she, I,* etc.). Usually an auxiliary verb follows (*is, do, did, can,* etc.). Informally, many Americans use the object pronoun (*him, her, me,* etc.) after *than*. An auxiliary verb does not follow.

EXERCISE 8 **Circle the correct words to complete the statement.**

EXAMPLE Chicago has (*more* / *less*) crime than San Francisco.

1. Chicago has a (*larger* / *smaller*) population than San Francisco.

2. Chicago is a (*safer* / *more dangerous*) place to live than San Francisco.

3. Houses in Chicago are (*more expensive* / *less expensive*) than houses in San Francisco.

4. Winter in Chicago is (*better* / *worse*) than winter in San Francisco.

5. Chicago has (*more* / *less*) rain than San Francisco.

EXERCISE 9 **ABOUT YOU** Compare yourself to another person, or compare two people you know using these adjectives.

EXAMPLES tall
I'm taller than my father.

talkative
My mother is more talkative than my father.

1. tall	5. thin	9. successful
2. educated	6. quiet	10. strong
3. friendly	7. stubborn	11. nervous
4. lazy	8. patient	12. polite

EXERCISE 10 Compare adults and children. Talk in general terms. You may discuss your answers.

EXAMPLE responsible
Adults are more responsible than kids.

1. polite	4. playful	7. shy
2. strong	5. sweet	8. patient
3. imaginative	6. friendly	9. serious

EXERCISE 11 Compare the city you live in now to another city you know.

EXAMPLES big
Tokyo is bigger than Boston.

crowded
Tokyo is more crowded than Boston.

1. crowded	4. noisy	7. cold in winter
2. modern	5. beautiful	8. dirty
3. small	6. interesting	9. sunny

12.6 Word Order with Comparisons

EXAMPLES	EXPLANATION
Houses in San Francisco **are more expensive** than houses in Chicago. I want to move to a **warmer climate**.	Put comparative adjectives **after** the verb *be* or **before** a noun.
The Hispanic population **is growing more quickly** than the African-American population.	Put comparative adverbs **after** the verb (phrase).
It **rains more** in Chicago. It **snows more** in Chicago.	Put *more, less, better,* and *worse* **after** a verb.
San Francisco has **more sunshine** than Chicago. San Francisco has **less pollution**.	Put *more, less, fewer, better,* and *worse* **before** a noun.

EXERCISE 12 **Compare yourself to another person, or compare two people you know using these verb phrases.**

EXAMPLES work hard
My mom works harder than my dad.

talk a lot
My brother talks more than my sister.

1. talk fast
2. gossip a lot
3. worry a lot
4. speak English fluently

5. work hard
6. drive carefully
7. spend a lot on clothes
8. make decisions quickly

EXERCISE 13 **Compare this city to another city you know. Use *better, worse, fewer, less,* or *more*.**

EXAMPLES factories
Chicago has more factories than Ponce.

public transportation
Moscow has better public transportation than Los Angeles.

1. traffic
2. people
3. rain
4. crime

5. pollution
6. sunshine
7. factories
8. snow

9. apartment buildings
10. job opportunities
11. tall buildings
12. homeless people

EXERCISE **14** **Make comparisons with the following words. Give your reasons. You may work with a partner or in a small group.**

EXAMPLE   men/women—have an easy life <u>In my opinion, men have an easier life than</u> <u>women. Women have to work two jobs—in the office and at home.</u>

1. men/women—have responsibilities _____

_____

2. American women/women in my native culture—have an easy life

_____

_____

3. married men/single men—are responsible _____

_____

4. American teenagers/teenagers in my native culture—have freedom

_____

_____

5. American teenagers/teenagers in my native culture—have

responsibilities _____

_____

6. American children/children in my native culture—have toys _____

_____

7. American children/children in my native culture—have a good

education _____

_____

8. American teachers/teachers in my native culture—get respect

_____

_____

EXERCISE **15** **Fill in the blanks with the comparative or superlative form of the word in parentheses ( ). Include *than* or *the* where necessary.**

EXAMPLES   August is usually ___<u>hotter than</u>___ May in Chicago.
                                     (hot)

January is usually ___<u>the coldest</u>___ month of the year in Chicago.
                                     (cold)

1. Los Angeles is _____ San Francisco.
                        (warm)

2. Seattle is _____ city in Washington.
                   (big)

3. The state of Hawaii is _____ south in the U.S.
(far)

4. Mexico City is _____ New York City.
(crowded)

5. New York City is _____ Los Angeles.
(crowded)

6. Mexico City is one of _____ cities in the world.
(crowded)

7. San Francisco is one of _____ cities in the U.S.
(beautiful)

8. _____ building in the world is not in the U.S.
(tall)

EXERCISE **16** **Two students in Seattle are talking. Fill in the blanks with appropriate words to make comparatives and superlatives.**

CD 2, TR 26

A: I'm planning to visit Chicago.

B: You're going to love it. It's a beautiful city. In fact, it's one of ___the most beautiful___ cities in the U.S.
(example)

A: It's the second largest city, isn't it?

B: Not anymore. Los Angeles is now _____ Chicago.
(1)

A: What should I see while I'm there?

B: You can visit the Willis Tower. It's _____ building in
(2)
the U.S. It has 110 stories. On a clear day, you can see for many miles.

A: Did you go to the top when you were there?

B: When I was there, the weather was bad. It was raining. I hope you

have _____ weather than I had. When are you going?
(3)

A: In August.

B: Ugh! August is the _____ month of the year. It's often 90
(4)
degrees or more. If you get hot, you can always go to the beach and cool off.

A: Is Chicago near an ocean?

B: No. It's near Lake Michigan.

A: Is it big like Lake Washington?

B: It's much _____ than Lake Washington. In fact, it's
(5)
one of the _____ lakes in the U.S.
(6)

(continued)

A: Is Chicago very rainy?

B: Not in the summer. It's sunny. In fact, it's much _____ (7) than Seattle.

A: What do you suggest that I see?

B: You should see the famous architecture downtown. The _____ (8) architects in the U.S. designed buildings in Chicago.

A: Do I need to take taxis everywhere, or does Chicago have a good public transportation system?

B: Taxis are so expensive! They're much _____ (9) than the buses and trains. You should use the public transportation. But remember that there's a lot of crime in Chicago, so it's not safe to travel alone at night. It's _____ (10) in the daytime.

A: Does Chicago have _____ (11) crime than Seattle?

B: Yes. But if you're careful, you'll be OK. I'm sure you'll enjoy it. It's an interesting place because it has people from all over the world. In fact, I think it's one of _____ (12) cities in the U.S.

Chicago skyline

Summary of Lesson 12

1. Adjectives

SHORT ADJECTIVES

Chicago is a **big** city.
Chicago is **bigger than** Boston.
New York is **the biggest** city in the U.S.

LONG ADJECTIVES

Houston is a **populated** city.
Chicago is **more populated than** Houston.
New York is **the most populated** city in the U.S.

2. Adverbs

SHORT ADVERBS

She walks **fast**.
She walks **faster than** her husband.
Her son walks **the fastest** in the family.

-LY ADVERBS

You speak English **fluently**.
You speak English **more fluently than** your brother.
Your sister speaks English **the most fluently** in your family.

3. Word Order

VERB (PHRASE) + COMPARATIVE ADVERB

She **speaks English more fluently** than her husband.
She **talks more** than her husband.

COMPARATIVE ADJECTIVE + NOUN

She has **more experience** than her husband.
She has a **better accent** than her sister.

Editing Advice

1. Don't use a comparison word when there is no comparison.

California is a ~~bigger~~ state.

2. Don't use *more* and *-er* together.

My new car is ~~more~~ better than my old one.

3. Use *than* before the second item in a comparison.

than
He is younger ~~that~~ his wife.

4. Use *the* before a superlative form.

the
China has biggest population in the world.
^

5. Use a plural noun after the phrase "one of the."

s
Jim is one of the tallest boy in the class.
^

6. Use the correct word order.

drives faster
She ~~faster drives~~ than her husband.

more
I have responsibilities ~~more~~ than you.
^

person
My uncle is the ~~person~~ most interesting in my family.
^

7. Don't use *the* with a possessive form.

My ~~the~~ best friend lives in London.

8. Use correct spelling.

happier
She is ~~happyer~~ than her friend.

Editing Quiz

Some of the shaded words and phrases have mistakes. Find the mistakes and correct them. If the shaded words are correct, write C.

I used to live in Mexico City. Now I live in St. Louis. These cities are

C
very different. Mexico City is *bigger* ~~more biger~~ than St. Louis. In fact, it's
(example)   *(example)*

one of the biggest city in the world. It's certainly the most large city in
(1)   *(2)*

Mexico. St. Louis has no mountains. Mexico City is surrounded by tall
(3)

mountains. I think Mexico City is prettyer that St. Louis. It has beautiful
(4)

parks. Mexico City is more interesting St. Louis. It has great museums.
(5)

But Mexico City has a few serious problems: it has more pollution than
(6)
St. Louis. My the oldest brother still lives there and he always complains
(7)
about the air quality. And I hate the subway. I think it's the more crowded
(8)
subway in the world.

No city is perfect. Each one has advantages and disadvantages. But my

heart is in Mexico City because my family and best friends live there.
(9)

Lesson 12 Test/Review

PART 1 **Find the mistakes with word order and correct them. Not every sentence has a mistake. If the sentence is correct, write C.**

EXAMPLES You more know about the U.S. than I do.
Soccer is more interesting than football for me.   *C*

1. I have problems more than you.

2. I earlier woke up than you.

3. Paris is the city most beautiful in the world.

4. She speaks English more fluently than her brother.

5. You faster type than I do.

6. My father is the most intelligent person in the family.

7. Your car is expensive more than my car.

8. You sing more beautifully than I do.

9. I travel more than my friend does.

10. You have more money than I do.

PART 2 **Fill in the blanks with the comparative or the superlative of the word in parentheses ( ). Add *the* or *than* if necessary.**

EXAMPLES New York City is _____ **bigger than** _____ Chicago.
                                    (big)

New York City is _____ **the biggest** _____ city in the U.S.
                                    (big)

1. Mount Everest is _____ mountain in the world.
                         (high)

2. A D grade is _____ a C grade.
                    (bad)

3. Johnson is one of _____ last names in the U.S.
   (common)

4. Tokyo is _____ Miami.
   (populated)

5. June 21 is _____ day of the year.
   (long)

6. The teacher speaks English _____ I do.
   (well)

7. Lake Superior is _____ lake in the U.S.
   (large)

8. Children learn a foreign language _____ adults.
   (quickly)

9. Do you think that Japanese cars are _____
   (good)

   American cars?

10. A dog is _____ a cat.
    (friendly)

11. Do you think women drive _____ men?
    (carefully)

12. Who is _____ student in this class?
    (good)

13. The teacher speaks English _____ I do.
    (fluently)

14. A dog is intelligent, but a monkey is _____.
    (intelligent)

Expansion

Classroom Activities

① **Form small groups of three to five students. Fill in the blanks to give information about yourself. Compare your list with the lists of other members of your group to make superlative statements.**

EXAMPLE Susana has the most relatives in this city.

a. number of relatives I have in this city _____

b. my height _____

c. number of letters in my last name _____

d. number of sisters and brothers I have _____

e. number of hours I watch TV per week _____

f. number of hours I exercise per week _____

g. money I spent today _____

h. distance I travel to come to this school _____

i. cups of coffee I drank today _____

j. number of miles I usually drive or walk per day _____

k. number of movies I usually see per year _____

❷ Work with a partner from the same native culture, if possible. Compare American men and men from your native culture. Compare American women and women from your native culture. Report some of your ideas to the class.

❸ Find a partner. Choose one of the following pairs and decide which of the two is better. Write five reasons why it is better. One person will make a statement saying that one is better than the other. The other person will follow with, "Yes, but . . ." and give another point of view.

EXAMPLE **A:** I think dogs are better pets than cats. They are more loyal.
B: Yes, but dogs need more attention.

- cats and dogs
- travel by train and travel by plane
- houses and condos
- spring and fall
- voice mail and answering machines
- leaving a spoken message or a text message

Talk
About It

❶ In your opinion, what is the biggest problem in the U.S. today?

❷ Talk about the advantages and disadvantages of living in a big city. Compare a big city to a small city or town.

❸ In choosing where to live, what is the most important thing to consider?

Write

About It

❶ Write about the biggest problem in the world today. Why is this a problem? How can we solve the problem?

❷ Choose one of the following topics to write a comparison:

a. Compare your present car with your previous car.

b. Compare two cities you know well.

c. Compare American women and women in your native culture.

d. Compare American men and men in your native culture.

e. Compare soccer and American football.

f. Compare your life in the U.S. and your life in your native country.

g. Compare a place where you lived before with the place where you live now.

Quito and Chicago

I am from Quito, Ecuador. I lived there for 21 years before I came to Chicago. There are many differences between Quito and Chicago. One difference is the climate. In Quito, the temperature is almost the same all year. The summers in Chicago are much hotter and the winters are much colder than in Quito. Another difference is the altitude. Chicago is at sea level and Quito is high in the mountains . . .

 For more practice using grammar in context, please visit our Web site.

Lesson

13

Grammar
**Auxiliary Verbs with
Too and *Either***

**Auxiliary Verbs in
Tag Questions**

Context
Dating and Marriage

Dating and Marriage

1. How is dating different from marriage?

2. Do American married couples spend more or less time together than couples in your native culture?

CD 2, TR 27

Read the following magazine article. Pay special attention to auxiliary verbs and *too* and *either*.

Most married couples want to spend time together, but the busy American lifestyle often doesn't allow it.

Meg and Don are a typical American couple.

Before Meg and Don met, they were both lonely. Meg wanted to get married, and Don **did too**. Meg believed that marriage would mean a lot of togetherness, and Don **did too**. When they were dating, Don didn't get together with friends very often, and Meg **didn't either**. They spent all their free time together. They discovered they had a lot in common.

A year after they met, they decided to get married. As they planned their wedding, they discovered their first differences while making decisions about their wedding: Meg wanted a big wedding, but Don **didn't**. Meg wanted an outdoor wedding, but Don **didn't**. They solved their differences by having a big indoor wedding.

As a married couple, they are now facing the realities of busy schedules and different interests. Don works hard, and Meg **does too**. They often have to work overtime. Don likes to cook, and Meg **does too**, but they rarely have time to do it. They often bring home carry-out dinners or eat in fast-food restaurants. On weekends, Don likes to go fishing, but Meg **doesn't**. So Don takes fishing trips with his friends. Meg likes to go to movies, but Don **doesn't**. He prefers to stay home and watch TV when he comes home from work. Both of them are planning to take college courses soon, which will give them even less time together.

So how do they solve these differences and stay close as a married couple? Once a month, they invite friends over on a weekend to have dinner and watch a movie or a football game on TV. When Don goes on a fishing trip, Meg gets together with her best friend and they go to a movie. That way, Don enjoys himself, and Meg **does too**.

Even though the realities of marriage are different from the romance of dating, Meg and Don are finding ways to adjust to married life.

13.1 Auxiliary Verbs with *Too* and *Either*

The auxiliary verbs are *do, does, did*, the modals, and *be*. We use auxiliary verbs with *too* and *either* to show similarity and avoid repetition of the same verb phrase.

EXAMPLES	EXPLANATION
Don is busy, and Meg **is too**. Don likes to cook, and Meg **does too**. Don was lonely, and Meg **was too**. Don lived alone, and Meg **did too**.	For affirmative statements, use the auxiliary verb + *too*.
Don doesn't have much free time, and Meg **doesn't either**. Don didn't get together with friends very often, and **Meg didn't either**.	For negative statements, use the auxiliary verb + *either*.
Don: I like to cook. *Meg*: **Me too**. *Don*: I don't have much time. *Meg*: **Me neither**.	In informal speech, we often say *me too* and *me neither*.
American: Meg has a hard job, and Don **does too**. **British:** Meg has a hard job, and Don **has too**.	When *have* is the main verb, Americans usually use *do, does, did* as a substitute. The British often use *have, has,* or *had*.

EXERCISE **1** Fill in the blanks with an auxiliary verb + *too* to show what Meg and Don have in common. Make sure that you use the same tense as the main verb.

EXAMPLE Don likes to cook, and Meg _____ does too _____.

1. Don has a hard job, and Meg _____.
2. Don is a hard worker, and Meg _____.
3. Don will take some college courses next semester, and Meg _____.
4. Don was lonely before, and Meg _____.
5. Don worked last Saturday, and Meg _____.

EXERCISE **2** Fill in the blanks with an auxiliary verb + *either* to show what Meg and Don have in common. Make sure you use the same tense as the main verb.

EXAMPLE Don doesn't like fast food, and Meg _____ doesn't either _____.

1. Don didn't finish college, and Meg _____.
2. Don isn't interested in baseball, and Meg _____.

3. Don doesn't have much free time, and Meg _____.

4. Don can't find time to cook, and Meg _____.

5. Don doesn't have any brothers or sisters, and Meg _____.

13.2 Auxiliary Verbs with Opposite Statements

We can use auxiliary verbs to show contrast and avoid repetition of the same verb phrase.

EXAMPLES	EXPLANATION
Don likes to go fishing, **but** Meg **doesn't**. Don is happy watching TV, **but** Meg **isn't**. Don doesn't like to go to movies, **but** Meg **does**. Don didn't want to have a big wedding, **but** Meg **did**.	We can use *but* to connect opposite statements. We often put a comma before *but*.
Meg: I want a big wedding. **Don:** I **don't**. **Meg:** I'm not interested in sports. **Don:** I **am**.	In conversation, we don't need *but* when one person says the opposite of another.

EXERCISE **3** **Fill in the blanks with an auxiliary verb to show what Meg and Don don't have in common.**

EXAMPLES Don likes to go fishing, but Meg __*doesn't*__.

1. Meg likes to go to movies, but Don _____.

2. Meg doesn't like to watch football on TV, but Don _____.

3. Meg reads when she has free time, but Don _____.

4. Don wanted to have a small wedding, but Meg _____.

5. Meg is interested in politics, but Don _____.

6. Meg isn't interested in cars, but Don _____.

7. Meg can play the piano, but Don _____.

EXERCISE **4** **Fill in the blanks to compare the U.S. and another country you know. Use *and . . . too* or *and . . . either* for similarities between the U.S. and the other country. Use *but* for differences. Use an auxiliary verb in all cases.**

EXAMPLE The U.S. is a big country, _____ *and Russia is too.* _____

OR

The U.S. is a big country, _____ *but Cuba isn't.* _____

1. The U.S. has more than 300 million people, _____

_____

2. The U.S. is in North America, _____

3. The U.S. has a president, _____

4. The U.S. doesn't have a prime minister, _____
_____

5. The U.S. fought in World War II, _____

6. The U.S. was a colony of England, _____

7. Americans like football, _____

8. Americans don't celebrate Labor Day in May, _____
_____

9. American public schools are closed on December 25, _____
_____

10. The U.S. has a presidential election every four years, _____
_____

EXERCISE 5 **ABOUT YOU** Check (✓) *yes* or *no* to tell what is true for you.
**Exchange your book with another student. Make statements about
you and the other student.**

EXAMPLE I don't speak Spanish, but Luis does.

	Yes	No
1. I speak Spanish.		
2. I'm interested in football.		
3. I'm interested in soccer.		
4. I have a car.		
5. I use the Internet every day.		
6. I can drive.		
7. I plan to move to another city.		
8. I'm going to buy a computer this year.		
9. I would like to visit Paris.		
10. I exercise every day.		
11. I'm studying math this semester.		
12. I studied English when I was in elementary school.		
13. I finished high school.		
14. I'm a vegetarian.		

EXERCISE 6 **Fill in the blanks in the conversation below. Use an auxiliary verb and *too* or *either* when necessary.**

CD 2, TR 28

A: I'm moving on Saturday. Maybe you and your brother can help me.

Are you working on Saturday?

B: My brother is working on Saturday, but I <u>'m not</u>.
(example)

I can help you.

A: I need a van. Do you have one?

B: I don't have one, but my brother _____. I'll ask him
(1)

if we can use it. By the way, why are you moving?

A: There are a couple of reasons. I got married recently. I like the

apartment, but my wife _____. She says it's too small for
(2)

two people.

B: How many rooms does your new apartment have?

A: The old apartment has two bedrooms, and the new one

_____. But the rooms are much bigger in the new one,
(3)

and there are more closets. Also, we'd like to live near the lake.

B: I _____, but apartments there are very expensive.
(4)

A: We found a nice apartment that isn't so expensive. Also, I'd like to own

a dog, but my present landlord doesn't permit pets.

B: Mine doesn't _____. What kind of dog do you plan
(5)

to get?

A: I like big watchdogs. Maybe a German Shepherd or a Doberman.

I don't like small dogs, but my wife _____.
(6)

B: I don't like small dogs either. They just make a lot of noise.

A: So now you know my reasons for moving. Can I count on you

for Saturday?

B: Of course you can.

13.3 Tag Questions

EXAMPLES	EXPLANATION
Married life is hard, **isn't it**? You don't like to go fishing, **do you**? Meg and Don work hard, **don't they**? Americans don't have much free time, **do they**?	A tag question is a short question that we put at the end of a statement. Use a tag question to ask if your statement is correct or if the listener agrees with you. The tag question uses an auxiliary verb in the same tense as the main verb.

Saturday with Meg and Don

Before
You Read

1. When families talk about "quality time," what do you think they mean?

2. What do you like to do in your free time?

CD 2, TR 29

Read the following conversation between Meg (M) and Don (D). Pay special attention to tag questions.

M: Would you like to go out to a movie tonight?

D: Not really.

M: Before we got married, you always wanted to go to movies, **didn't you**?

D: I suppose so. But I'm tired now. I'd rather stay home and watch TV or rent a movie.

M: You're always tired, **aren't you**?

D: Well, actually, yes. I work hard all week, and now I just want to relax.

M: When we got married, we planned to spend a lot of time together, **didn't we**?

D: I know. But married life is hard. Besides, we spend a lot of time together on weekends, **don't we**?

M: Yes, we do. We go shopping, we do the laundry, we visit your parents, we cut the grass, we clean the house. But we don't have any fun together anymore, **do we**?

(continued)

D: Fishing is fun for me. Next weekend I'm going fishing with my buddies. But you don't like fishing, **do you**?

M: Not really.

D: Before we got married, you said you'd try fishing with me, **didn't you**?

M: Yes, I did. But I was just trying to please you then. I realize I like to eat fish, but I don't like to catch them.

D: Well, somebody has to catch them if you want to eat them.

M: But we never eat them because we don't have time to cook. Now that it's Saturday, we're both too tired to cook. What are we going to do for dinner tonight?

D: We can get some carry-out from that new Chinese place nearby, **can't we**?

M: I suppose so.

D: You're not happy, **are you**?

M: That's not true! I love you, but I just want to spend more "quality time" with you.

D: I have an idea. Let's invite some friends over next weekend, and we can make our special fish recipe for them. That will be fun, **won't it**?

M: That's a great idea.

13.4 Auxiliary Verbs in Tag Questions

AFFIRMATIVE STATEMENTS	NEGATIVE TAG QUESTIONS	EXPLANATION
Don likes fishing,	**doesn't** he?	An affirmative statement has a negative tag question. Make a contraction with the auxiliary verb + *not* and then use a subject pronoun.
You're always tired,	**aren't** you?	
We can eat out,	**can't** we?	
We planned to spend time together,	**didn't** we?	
Meg is unhappy,	**isn't** she?	
NEGATIVE STATEMENTS	AFFIRMATIVE TAG QUESTIONS	EXPLANATION
You aren't happy,	**are you**?	A negative statement has an affirmative tag question. Use the auxiliary verb + a subject pronoun.
You don't like fishing,	**do you**?	
We never have fun together anymore,	**do we**?	

Special Cases with Tag Questions

EXAMPLES	EXPLANATION
There isn't a lot of free time, **is there**? There are a lot of things to do, **aren't there**?	If the sentence begins with *there is* or *there are*, use *there* in the tag.
This is a typical marriage, **isn't it**? That will be fun, **won't it**?	If the sentence begins with *this* or *that*, use *it* in the tag.
These are normal problems, **aren't they**? Those romantic days are over, **aren't they**?	If the sentence begins with *these* or *those*, use *they* in the tag.
Informal: I'm right, **aren't I**? **Formal:** I'm right, **am I not**?	*Am I not*? is a very formal tag. Informally, we usually say *aren't I*?

EXERCISE 7 Add a tag question. All the statements are affirmative and have an auxiliary verb.

EXAMPLE   This class is large, _____ isn't it? _____

1. You're a foreign student, _____
2. You can understand English, _____
3. We'll have a test soon, _____
4. We should study, _____
5. There's a library at this school, _____
6. You'd like to improve your English, _____
7. This is an easy lesson, _____
8. I'm asking too many questions, _____

EXERCISE 8 Add a tag question. All the statements are negative and have an auxiliary verb.

EXAMPLE   You can't speak Italian, _____ can you? _____

1. You aren't an American citizen, _____
2. The teacher can't speak your language, _____
3. We shouldn't talk in the library, _____
4. You weren't absent yesterday, _____
5. There aren't any Japanese students in this class, _____
6. This exercise isn't hard, _____

EXERCISE **9**   Add a tag question. All the statements are affirmative. Substitute the main verb with an auxiliary verb in the tag question.

EXAMPLE   You have the textbook, _____*don't you?*_____

1. English has a lot of irregular verbs, _____
2. You want to speak English well, _____
3. You understood the explanation, _____
4. You have a cell phone, _____
5. They bought a laptop last week, _____
6. We had a test last week, _____

EXERCISE **10**   Add a tag question. All the statements are negative.

EXAMPLE   We don't have class on Saturday, _____*do we?*_____

1. The teacher doesn't pronounce your name correctly, _____
2. Your brother didn't take the last test, _____
3. You didn't bring your dictionary today, _____
4. We don't always have homework, _____
5. I don't have your phone number, _____
6. Your mother doesn't speak English, _____

EXERCISE **11**   This is a conversation between two acquaintances,[1] Bob (B) and Sam (S). Sam can't remember where he met Bob. Fill in the blanks with a tag question.

CD 2, TR 30

B: Hi, Sam.

S: Uh, hi . . .

B: You don't remember me, _____*do you?*_____
                                 (example)

S: You look familiar, but I can't remember your name. We were in the

same chemistry class last semester, _____
                                     (1)

B: No.

S: Then we probably met in math class, _____
                                           (2)

B: Wrong again. I'm Meg Wilson's brother.

S: Now I remember you. Meg introduced us at a party last summer,

_____? And your name is Bob, _____
        (3)   *(4)*

[1]An *acquaintance* is a person you don't know well.

B: That's right.

S: How are you, Bob? You graduated last year, _____
(5)

B: Yes. And I've got a good job now.

S: You majored in computers, _____
(6)

B: Yes. But I decided to go into real estate.

S: And how's your sister Meg? I never see her anymore. She moved back to California, _____
(7)

B: No. She's still here. But she's married now, and she's very busy.

S: Who did she marry?

B: Don Tripton. You met him, _____
(8)

S: Yes, I think so. Say hello to Meg when you see her. It was great seeing you again, Bob.

EXERCISE 12 **A mother (M) is talking to her daughter (D). Fill in the blanks with a tag question.**

M: You didn't get your scholarship, _did you?_
(example)

D: How did you know?

M: Well, you look very disappointed. You can apply again next year, _____?
(1)

D: Yes. But what will I do this year?

M: There are government loans, _____?
(2)

D: Yes.

M: And you don't have to pay them back until you graduate, _____?
(3)

D: No.

M: And your professors will give you letters of recommendation, _____?
(4)

D: I'm sure they will.

M: So don't worry. Just try to get a loan, and you can apply again next year for a scholarship.

13.5 Answering a Tag Question

STATEMENT WITH TAG QUESTION	SHORT ANSWER	EXPLANATION
Meg and Don are married now, **aren't they**? They work hard, **don't they**?	**Yes**, they are. **Yes**, they do.	When we use a negative tag, we expect the answer to be *yes*.
They don't have much free time, **do they**? Meg doesn't like to go fishing, **does she**?	**No**, they don't. **No**, she doesn't.	When we use an affirmative tag, we expect the answer to be *no*.
Don: You aren't happy, **are you**? *Meg:* You like to go to movies, **don't you**?	*Meg:* **Yes**, I am. I love you. *Don:* **No**, I don't. I like to stay home and watch TV.	Answering *yes* to an affirmative tag shows disagreement. Answering *no* to a negative tag shows disagreement.

EXERCISE 13 Complete the answer in the left column. Then check the meaning of the answer in the right column. You may work with a partner.

A: You don't have a car, do you? **B:** Yes, <u> I do. </u> *(example)*	✓ Person B has a car. Person B doesn't have a car.
A: You aren't married, are you? **B:** No, <u> </u> *(1)*	Person B is married. Person B isn't married.
A: You don't like this city, do you? **B:** No, <u> </u> *(2)*	Person B likes this city. Person B doesn't like this city.
A: You don't have a watch, do you? **B:** Yes, <u> </u> *(3)*	Person B has a watch. Person B doesn't have a watch.
A: You don't speak Russian, do you? **B:** No, <u> </u> *(4)*	Person B speaks Russian. Person B doesn't speak Russian.
A: You can drive, can't you? **B:** No, <u> </u> *(5)*	Person B can drive. Person B can't drive.
A: The U.S. is the biggest country in the world, isn't it? **B:** No, <u> </u> *(6)*	Person B agrees with the statement. Person B doesn't agree with the statement.
A: You work on Saturday, don't you? **B:** Yes, <u> </u> *(7)*	Person B works on Saturday. Person B doesn't work on Saturday.

EXERCISE 14 **Read a statement to another student and add a tag question. The other student will tell you if this information is correct or not.**

EXAMPLES You speak Polish, _____don't you?_____
No, I don't. I speak Ukrainian.

You aren't from Poland, _____are you?_____
No, I'm not. I'm from Ukraine.

You came to the U.S. two years ago, _____didn't you?_____
Yes, I did.

1. You're not married, _____

2. You have a cell phone, _____

3. You didn't study English in elementary school, _____

4. You have the textbook, _____

5. You don't live alone, _____

6. You'll take another English course next semester, _____

7. You won't graduate this year, _____

8. You took the last test, _____

9. You have to work on Saturday, _____

10. The teacher doesn't speak your language, _____

11. You can drive, _____

12. This class isn't too hard for you, _____

13. There was a test last Friday, _____

14. You don't speak German, _____

15. I'm asking you a lot of personal questions, _____

EXERCISE 15 **Fill in the blanks with a tag question and an answer that tells if the information is true or not.**

A: You come from Russia, _____don't you?_____
                                    (example)
B: _____. I come from Ukraine.
      (1)
A: They speak Polish in Ukraine, _____
                                        (2)
B: _____. They speak Ukrainian and Russian.
      (3)
A: Ukraine isn't part of Russia, _____
                                        (4)
B: _____. Ukraine and Russia are different. They were
      (5)
both part of the former Soviet Union.

A: You come from a big city, _____
                                    (6)

(continued)

B: _____. I come from Kiev. It's the capital of Ukraine.
(7)
It's very big.

A: Your parents aren't here, _____
(8)

B: _____. We came together two years ago. I live with them.
(9)

A: You studied English in your country, _____
(10)

B: _____. I studied only Russian and German. I never
(11)
studied English there.

A: You're not going to go back to live in your country, _____
(12)

B: _____. I'm an immigrant here. I plan to become an
(13)
American citizen.

EXERCISE 16 **This is a conversation between Meg (M) and her best friend, Lydia (L). Fill in the blanks with tag questions and answers.**

CD 2, TR 31

M: Hello?

L: Hi, Meg. This is Lydia.

M: Oh, hi, Lydia.

L: Can you talk? I hear the TV in the background. Don's home, _isn't he?_
(example)

M: _____, he _____. He's watching TV, as usual.
(1)   (2)

L: Are you busy?

M: I'm always busy, _____?
(3)

L: Well, _____, you _____.
(4)   (5)

M: But I can make some time for you. What's up?

L: I have a new boyfriend. His name is Peter.

M: But you're dating Michael, _____?
(6)

L: _____. Not anymore. We broke up a month ago.
(7)
The last time I talked to you was over a month ago, _____?
(8)

M: Over a month ago? That's terrible. We used to talk every day.

L: Now that you're married, you don't have much free time anymore,

_____?
(9)

M: _____, I _____. I almost never have time for myself anymore.
    (10)   (11)
Or for my friends. Tell me about your new boyfriend.

L: We have so much in common. We both like sports, the same kind of music, the same kind of food. . . . If we get married, we'll have the rest of our lives to have fun together.

M: You're not thinking of getting married, _____?
    (12)

L: _____. Not yet. I'm just dreaming.
    (13)

M: Dating is so much fun, _____?
    (14)

L: _____, it _____. But marriage isn't, _____?
    (15)   (16)   (17)

M: "Fun" is not a word that describes marriage.

L: But you had a lot of fun with Don before you got married, _____?
    (18)

M: _____, we _____. But things changed after the wedding.
    (19)   (20)
Now all we do together is laundry, shopping, and cleaning.

L: That doesn't sound very interesting. But there are good things about being married, _____?
    (21)

M: Of course. Don's my best friend. We help each other with all our problems.

L: Before you got married, I was your best friend, _____?
    (22)
But now I almost never see you.

M: You're right, Lydia. I'll try harder to call you more often.

Summary of Lesson 13

1. Use auxiliary verbs to avoid repetition of the same verb phrase.

AFFIRMATIVE	AND	SHORTENED AFFIRMATIVE + *TOO*
Meg has a job,	and	Don does too.
Meg is busy,	and	Don is too.

NEGATIVE	AND	SHORTENED NEGATIVE + *EITHER*
Meg doesn't work on Saturdays,	and	Don doesn't either.
Meg can't find free time,	and	Don can't either.

AFFIRMATIVE	BUT	SHORTENED NEGATIVE
Meg finished college,	but	Don didn't.
Don likes fishing,	but	Meg doesn't.

NEGATIVE	BUT	SHORTENED AFFIRMATIVE
Don doesn't like movies,	but	Meg does.
Don didn't want a big wedding,	but	Meg did.

2. Use auxiliary verbs in tag questions.

AFFIRMATIVE	NEGATIVE TAG
You're busy now,	aren't you?
We have a hard life,	don't we?
There are a lot of things to do,	aren't there?

NEGATIVE	AFFIRMATIVE TAG
You don't like fishing,	do you?
I can't go fishing alone,	can I?
We never have time together,	do we?

Editing Advice

1. Don't omit the auxiliary from a shortened sentence with *too* or *either*.

      do
My brother has a new house, and I too.

      didn't
John didn't take the test, and I either.

2. Don't confuse *too* and *either*.

                                     either
Jack doesn't speak French, and his wife doesn't ~~too~~.

3. If half your sentence is negative and half is affirmative, the connecting word is *but*, not *and*.

                        but
He doesn't speak French, ~~and~~ his wife does.

4. Be careful to answer a tag question correctly.

                                   No
New York isn't the capital of the U.S., is it? ~~Yes~~, it isn't.

5. Use a pronoun (or *there*) in the tag question.

                    it
That's your hat, isn't ~~that~~?

                                    there
There's some milk in the refrigerator, isn't ~~it~~?

6. Be careful to use the correct auxiliary verb and the correct tense.

                              did
Her sister didn't go to the party, ~~does~~ she?

                                will
She won't go back to her country, ~~does~~ she?

Editing Quiz

Don is calling Meg on her cell phone. Some of the shaded words and phrases have mistakes. Find the mistakes and correct them. If the shaded words are correct, write C.

D: Hi, Meg.

M: Hi, Don. What's up?

D: Some friends are coming over this afternoon to watch the football game.
I told you, ~~didn't I~~? You remember, ~~do you~~?
    C (example)   *don't you* (example)

M: Of course I am.
    (1)

D: Can you pick up some things before you come home?

M: I think we have enough food at home. We have snacks, aren't we?
    (2)

D: Yes, we do. But we don't have any cheese and crackers, don't we?
    (3)   (4)

M: Yes, we don't. I'll get some. Who's coming tonight?
    (5)

D: Sam called today. He's coming, but Nancy doesn't.
    (6)

M: Why not?

D: They can't find a babysitter for their daughter, Pam.

M: Tell them to bring their daughter. Pam's eight and Sofie does, too.
    (7)
    I'm sure they can find something to do together.

D: But Sofie has a violin lesson this afternoon, doesn't she?
    (8)

M: That's tomorrow, not today. I sure hope Sam's wife is coming. We can
    watch a movie while you guys watch football. She doesn't like football,
    and I too.
    (9)

D: How do you know? You never even watch football.

M: Don't you remember? I tried to watch football with you guys last time, and
    Nancy was too, but we just saw a bunch of guys falling on top of each other.
    (10)

D: You can understand it if you try, can't you?
    (11)

M: If I try. But the point is that I don't want to try.

Lesson 13 Test/Review

PART 1 This is a conversation between two students who are meeting for the first time. Fill in the blanks with an auxiliary verb to complete this conversation. Use *either* or *too* when necessary.

C: Hi. My name is Carlos. I'm a new student.

E: I _____am too_____. My name is Elena.
(example)

C: I come from Mexico.

E: Oh, really? I _____. I come from a small town in the
(1)
northern part of Mexico.

C: I come from Mexico City. I love big cities.

E: I _____. I prefer small towns.
(2)

C: How do you like living here in Los Angeles?

E: I don't like it much, but my sister _____. She has a
(3)
good job, but I _____. I miss my job back home.
(4)

C: I love it here, and my family _____. The climate is
(5)
similar to the climate of Mexico City.

E: What about the air quality? Mexico City doesn't have clean air, and
Los Angeles _____, so you probably feel right at home.
(6)

C: Ha! You're right about the air quality, but there are many nice things
about Los Angeles. Would you want to get a cup of coffee and continue
this conversation? I don't have any more classes today.

E: Yes, I _____, but I have to go home now. I enjoyed
(7)
our talk.

C: I _____. Maybe we can continue it some other time.
(8)
Well, see you in class tomorrow.

PART **2**   In this conversation, a new student is trying to find out information about the school and class. Add a tag question.

A: There's a parking lot at the school, _____isn't there?_____
(example)

B: Yes. It's east of the building.

A: The teacher's American, _____
_(1)_

B: Yes, she is.

A: She doesn't give hard tests, _____
_(2)_

B: Not too easy, not too hard.

A: We'll have a day off for Christmas, _____
_(3)_

B: We'll have a whole week off.

A: We have to write compositions, _____
_(4)_

B: A few.

A: And we can't use a dictionary when we write a composition,

_____
_(5)_

B: Who told you that? Of course we can. You're very nervous about

school, _____
_(6)_

A: Yes, I am. It isn't easy to learn a new language, _____
_(7)_

B: No.

A: And I should ask questions about things I want to know,

_____
_(8)_

B: Yes, of course. You don't have any more questions, _____
_(9)_

A: No.

B: Well, I'll see you in the next class. Bye.

Expansion

Classroom Activities

1 Complete each statement. Then find a partner and compare yourself to your partner by using an auxiliary verb.

EXAMPLES   **A:** I speak _Chinese_.

           B: I do too. OR I don't.

           A: I don't speak _Spanish_.

           B: I don't either. OR I do.

   a. I speak _____.

   b. I don't speak _____.

   c. I can _____.

   d. I have _____.

   e. I don't have _____.

   f. I'm _____.

   g. I usually drink _____ every day.

   h. I'm going to _____ next week.

   i. I come from _____.

   j. I'm wearing _____ today.

   k. I bought _____ last week.

   l. I went _____ last week.

   m. I don't like _____.

   n. I brought _____ to the U.S.

   o. I don't like to eat _____.

   p. I can't _____ very well.

   q. I should _____ more.

❷ The teacher will read each statement. If the statement is true for you, stand up. Students will take turns making statements about any two classmates.

EXAMPLE   Teacher: Stand up if you drank coffee this morning.
             Student: I drank coffee this morning, and Tom did too.
                      Mario didn't drink coffee this morning, and Sofia didn't either.

Stand up if you . . .

- have more than five sisters and brothers
- walked to class today
- will graduate in the next two years
- are wearing running shoes
- have a photo of a family member in your pocket or bag
- want to review this lesson
- went to a movie last week
- can't swim
- plan to buy a car soon
- are tired now
- aren't married
- ate pizza today
- speak Polish
- don't like this game
- can understand American TV
- didn't take the last test

❸ Find a partner. Tell your partner some things that you think you know about him or her and about his or her native culture or country. Your partner will tell you if you are right or wrong.

EXAMPLES   The capital of your country is New Delhi, isn't it?
              Hindus don't eat beef, do they?
              You're studying engineering, aren't you?

❹ Tell the teacher what you think you know about the U.S. or Americans. You may work with a partner. The teacher will tell you if you're right or wrong.

EXAMPLES   Most Americans don't speak a foreign language, do they?
              Alaska is the largest state, isn't it?

1 Do you think young people have realistic expectations of marriage?

2 Some people say that opposites attract. Do you think that two people who are opposites in many ways can have a good marriage?

3 What do you think are the ingredients of a good marriage?

Write
About It

Choose two sports, countries, people, or stores and write sentences comparing them.

My Mother and My Father

My mother and my father have some things in common and some big differences too. My mother is the oldest of five children, and my father is too. So they both had a lot of responsibilities growing up. My father finished high school, but my mother didn't. My mother didn't have the opportunity. But they are both very intelligent . . .

For more practice using grammar in context, please visit our Web site.

Grammar
Verb Review

Context
Washington Interns

The Supreme Court, Washington, D.C.

Washington Interns

1. How can a college student get work experience?

2. What do most college students do during their summer break?

CD 2, TR 32

Read the information and e-mail that follows it. Pay special attention to verb tenses.

Some college students **want to find** interesting work and **gain** valuable experience over the summer. One way **is to work** as an intern in Washington, D.C. Interns **don't** get paid; the reward **comes** from the experience and knowledge they **gain**. Interns **learn** about the U.S. government and politics.

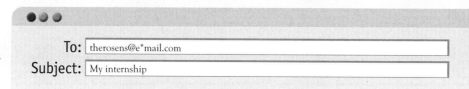

To: therosens@e*mail.com

Subject: My internship

Dear Mom and Dad,

I **can't** believe it! I**'m working** at the Supreme Court now. I**'m gaining** so much experience here. When I **go** to law school next year, I**'ll have** a much greater understanding of American law. And when I **apply** for a job, this internship **will look** really good on my résumé[1].

At first, I **felt** a little lost and lonely because I **didn't know** anyone. But that soon **changed**. Through my classes and job, I **meet** new and interesting people every day.

Besides my work, I**'m taking** classes at Georgetown University. My professors **are** great! I**'m learning** so much. My knowledge about American law **is increasing** greatly.

I **have** an interesting roommate, too. She**'s** from California. Her name **is** Nicole. She**'s working** at the Department of Education. She**'s planning** to become a teacher. We **have** a small but comfortable apartment. We **have to shop** and **make** our own meals. So besides learning about the Supreme Court, I**'m learning** how to cook. I**'m becoming** much more responsible. **Are** you surprised?

[1]A *résumé* is a document that lists job experience and education. A person looking for a job usually writes a résumé.

Whenever Nicole and I **have** free time, we **go** to see the interesting places in Washington. But we rarely **have** free time because of our jobs and our classes. We **might go** to the art museum this weekend if we **have** enough time.

There **is** one thing I **don't like**: I **have to wear** formal clothes every day. I **can't wear** jeans at my job. We **must look** very professional for work. I **didn't have** the right kind of clothes when I **arrived**, so I **went** shopping and **spent** about $500 on new clothes. I **hope** you **don't mind**. I **put** the charges on your credit card. As you **know**, I'**m not making** any money here. But **don't worry**. I promise I won't **spend** any more money on clothes.

When I **get** home, I'**ll tell** you much more about my experience this summer. I **know** I **should write** more often, but I just **don't have** the time.

Love,
Lena

FAQs (Frequently Asked Questions) About Washington Internships

- How **does** a student **get** an internship?

  Students **should contact** their senators or representatives to apply for an internship.

- What kind of work **do** interns **do**?

  They **work** in research, **help** plan events, **manage** databases, and **write** for newsletters.

- Where **do** they **live**?

  They **live** in on-campus apartments at nearby universities.

- **Do** they **have to take** classes?

  Yes, they **do**. And they **must participate** in other activities.

- How busy **is** their schedule?

  It **is** *very* busy. Interns **learn** about education, politics, and government.

- **Will** they **receive** college credit for the internship?

  Yes. They **will receive** six hours of college credit.

14.1 Verbs

Simple Present Tense

EXAMPLES	USES
Washington **is** the capital of the U.S. Some students **want** summer jobs. Some interns in Washington **take** classes at Georgetown University.	Facts
Interns students **have** vacation in the summer. Many American students **wear** jeans to class.	Customs and habits
Interns **take** classes every day. When they **have** free time, they **go** to interesting places.	Regular activities
I **have** a great roommate now. I **like** my job now.	With nonaction verbs
When I **get** home, I'll tell you more.	In a future time clause
If you **become** an intern in Washington, you will get valuable experience.	In a future *if* clause
My roommate **is** from California. She **comes** from San Diego.	With place of origin

Present Continuous Tense

EXAMPLES	EXPLANATION
Lena **is writing** a letter to her parents now.	Actions that are happening now
Lena **is learning** how to cook. She **isn't making** any money this summer.	Actions that are happening in a present time period

Future Tense

EXAMPLES	EXPLANATION
They **are going to return** to college in the fall. Nicole **is going to become** a teacher.	Plans for the future (use *be going to*)
I **will** never **forget** this experience. This experience **is going to help** me in my future.	Predictions (use *will* or *be going to*)
I'll write more later.	Promises (use *will*)

Simple Past Tense

EXAMPLES	EXPLANATION
I **went** shopping because I **needed** clothes. I **spent** $500 on clothes. I **used** your credit card.	Actions that happened at a specific time in the past

Be

EXAMPLES	EXPLANATION
Washington, D.C., **is** the capital of the U.S.	To classify or define the subject
Washington **is** interesting.	To describe the subject
The Supreme Court **is** in Washington.	To tell the location of the subject
Nicole **is** from San Diego.	With a place of origin
She **was born** in California.	With *born*
There **are** many government buildings in Washington.	With *there*

Modals

EXAMPLES	EXPLANATION
Lena **can** wear jeans to class. Lena **can** study at night.	Permission Ability
She **should** write to her parents more often. If you want more information about internships, you **should** write to your senator.	Advisability
She **must** look professional in her job. Interns **must** participate in activities.	Necessity
They **might** go to the art museum this weekend. Lena **may** visit Nicole in California next year.	Possibility

Infinitives

EXAMPLES	EXPLANATION
Lena wants **to have** an internship. It's important **to be** on time.	An infinitive doesn't show tense.

Imperatives

EXAMPLES	EXPLANATION
Write to me. **Don't worry** about me.	An imperative uses the base form. A negative imperative uses *don't* + base form.

EXERCISE 1 **Without looking at the reading on pages 398–399, fill in the blanks with the correct tense or form of the verb in parentheses ( ). Some answers may vary.**

I can't _**believe**_ it! I _____ at the Supreme Court now. I _____
(example: believe)   (1 work)   (2 gain)

so much experience here. When I _____ to law school next year,
(3 go)

I _____ a much greater understanding of American law. And when
(4 have)

I _____ for a job, this internship _____ really good on my résumé.
(5 apply)   (6 look)

At first, I _____ a little lost and lonely because I _____
(7 feel)   (8 not/know)

anyone. But that soon _____. Through my classes and job,
(9 change)

I _____ new and interesting people every day.
(10 meet)

Besides my work, I _____ classes at Georgetown University.
(11 take)

My professors _____ great! I _____ so much. My knowledge
(12 be)   (13 learn)

about American law _____ rapidly.
(14 increase)

I _____ an interesting roommate, too. She _____ from
(15 have)   (16 be)

California. Her name is Nicole. She _____ at the Department of
(17 work)

Education. She's planning to _____ a teacher. We _____ a small
(18 become)   (19 have)

but comfortable apartment. We have to _____ and _____ our
(20 shop)   (21 make)

own meals. So besides learning about the Supreme Court, I _____
(22 learn)

how to cook. I _____ much more responsible. Are you surprised?
(23 become)

Whenever Nicole and I _____ free time, we _____ to see
(24 have)   (25 go)

the interesting places in Washington. But we rarely _____ free time
(26 have)

because of our jobs and our classes. We might _____ to the art
(27 go)

museum this weekend if we _____ enough time.
(28 have)

There is one thing I don't like: I have to wear formal clothes every day.

I can't _____ blue jeans at my job. We must _____ very
(29 wear)   (30 look)

professional for our jobs. I _____ the right kind of clothes when I
(31 not/have)

_____, so I _____ shopping and _____ about $500 on
(32 arrive)   (33 go)   (34 spend)

new clothes. I hope you _____. I _____ the charges on your
                        (35 not/mind)   (36 put)

credit card. As you _____, I _____ any money here. But don't
                    (37 know)   (38 not/make)

_____. I promise I _____ any more money on clothes.
(39 worry)   (40 not/spend)

When I _____ home, I _____ you much more about my
       (41 get)   (42 tell)

experience this summer. I _____ I should _____ more often,
                         (43 know)   (44 write)

but I just _____ the time.
           (45 not/have)

Love,

Lena

14.2 Statements and Questions

Simple Present Tense

BASE FORM	-S FORM
Interns **wear** formal clothes.	Lena **lives** with a roommate.
They **don't wear** jeans.	She **doesn't live** alone.
Do they **wear** formal clothes to class?	**Does** she **live** in a dorm?
No, they **don't**.	No, she **doesn't**.
What **do** they **wear** to class?	Where **does** she **live**?
Why **don't** they **wear** jeans to work?	Why **doesn't** she **live** in a dorm?
How many students **wear** jeans?	Who **lives** in a dorm?

Present Continuous Tense

IS + VERB + ING	ARE + VERB + ING
Nicole **is planning** to become a teacher.	They **are taking** classes.
Lena **isn't planning** to become a teacher.	They **aren't taking** English classes.
Is she **planning** to teach in California?	**Are** they **taking** classes at Georgetown?
No, she **isn't**.	Yes, they **are**.
Where **is** she **planning** to teach?	What kind of classes **are** they **taking**?
Why **isn't** she **planning** to teach in California?	Why **aren't** they **taking** English classes?
Who **is planning** to teach in California?	How many students **are taking** classes?

Future Tense

WILL	BE GOING TO
They **will go** home at the end of the summer.	Lena **is going to buy** books.
They **won't go** on vacation.	She **isn't going to buy** more clothes.
Will they **go** back to college?	**Is** she **going to buy** a computer?
Yes, they **will**.	No, she **isn't**.
When **will** they **go** back to college?	What **is** she **going to buy**?
Why **won't** they **go** on vacation?	Why **isn't** she **going to buy** a computer?
Who **will go** back to college?	Who **is going to buy** a computer?

Simple Past Tense

REGULAR VERB	IRREGULAR VERB
She **used** her parents' credit card.	She **bought** new clothes.
She **didn't use** cash.	She **didn't buy** jeans.
Did she **use** their card a lot?	**Did** she **buy** formal clothes?
No, she **didn't**.	Yes, she **did**.
Why **did** she **use** their card?	Why **did** she **buy** formal clothes?
Why **didn't** she **use** cash?	Why **didn't** she **buy** jeans?
Who **used** the card?	Who **bought** formal clothes?

Be

PRESENT	PAST
They **are** in Washington, D.C.	Lena **was** lost at first.
They **aren't** at college.	She **wasn't** happy.
Are they in California?	**Was** she alone?
No, they **aren't**.	Yes, she **was**.
Why **are** they in Washington?	Why **was** she alone?
Why **aren't** they in California?	Why **wasn't** she happy?
Who **is** in California?	Who **was** alone?

Modals

CAN	SHOULD
She **can** wear jeans to class.	She **should** study every day.
She **can't** wear jeans to work.	She **shouldn't** go to parties every day.
Can she wear jeans at college?	**Should** she study history?
Yes, she **can**.	Yes, she **should**.
What **can** she wear?	What else **should** she study?
Why **can't** she wear jeans to work?	Why **shouldn't** she go to parties?
Who **can** wear jeans?	Who **should** study?

EXERCISE 2 **Fill in the blanks with the negative form of the underlined verb.**

EXAMPLE   Lena <u>is</u> in Washington this summer. She _____isn't_____ at home.

1. She<u>'s getting</u> experience. She _____ money for her work.

2. She <u>bought</u> new clothes. She _____ jeans.

3. She <u>writes</u> a lot for her classes. She _____ a lot of letters.

4. She<u>'ll finish</u> college next year. She _____ college this summer.

5. She<u>'s going to return</u> to college in the fall. She _____ to Washington next summer.

6. She <u>can wear</u> jeans to class. She _____ jeans to work.

7. She <u>must look</u> professional at work. She _____ informal at work.

EXERCISE 3 **Fill in the blanks with a question about interns, based on the responses that follow.**

EXAMPLES   <u>Do interns get money for their work?</u>

No, they don't. They get experience, not money.

<u>Will the internship end in September?</u>

No, it won't. The internship will end in August.

1. _____

   Yes, they do. They have to take classes.

2. _____

   No, they don't live in dorms. They live in apartments.

3. _____

   Yes, they are. They are very busy with classes, work, and activities.

4. _____

   Yes, they will. They will receive six hours of college credit.

5. _____

   No, she can't. Lena can't wear jeans to work.

6. _____

   Yes, she is. She's learning how to cook.

7. _____

   No, she didn't. She didn't know anyone when she arrived in Washington.

8. _____

Yes, she does. She works at the Supreme Court.

9. _____

Yes, she did. She bought some new clothes.

EXERCISE **4** **Write a question with the _wh-_ words given. Use the same tense. An answer is not necessary.**

EXAMPLE Lena is calling her mother. Why _is she calling her mother?_____

1. Lena will go home soon. When _____

_____

2. Her mother doesn't remember the roommate's name. Why _____

_____

3. Lena can't go home for a weekend. Why _____

_____

4. Lena doesn't have much money. How much money _____

_____

5. Lena is learning a lot this summer. What _____

_____

6. She doesn't have time to write letters. Why _____

_____

7. Lena went to Virginia last weekend. With whom _____

_____

8. Nicole comes from a different state. Where _____

_____ from?

9. Lena didn't cook before this summer. Why _____

_____

10. Someone went to Virginia. Who _____

_____

11. The internship will help Lena in the future. How _____

_____

12. She is working at a branch of the government. At which branch

_____

13. Lena felt lonely at first. Why _____

_____

14. She can't wear jeans to work. Why _____

_____

15. She must take classes. How many classes _____

_____

16. She is going to get college credits for her internship. How many credits

_____

17. Lena should call her parents more often. How often _____

_____

EXERCISE 5 Lena (L) is talking to her mother (M) on the phone. She is calling from Washington, D.C. Fill in the blanks with the correct form of the words in parentheses ( ).

M: Hello?

L: Hi, Mom. This is Lena.

M: Hi, Lena. I ___'m___ happy to _____
        (example: be)   (1 hear)
your voice. You _____. You just send short text messages.
                   (2 never/call)

L: I'm sorry, Mom. I _____ much time.
                           (3 not/have)

M: Why _____ time?
           (4 you/not/have)

L: I have to work, go to classes, and participate in activities all day.

Last weekend we _____ to Virginia.
                     (5 go)

M: Who _____?
           (6 drive)

L: No one. We _____ the Metro. Public transportation is
                   (7 use)
really good here.

M: _____ enough to eat this summer? Who
        (8 you/get)
_____ for you?
   (9 cook)

L: I _____ to _____ this summer.
        (10 learn)   (11 cook)
_____ surprised?
   (12 be/you)

M: Yes, I am. When you were home, you never _____.
                                                    (13 cook)
You _____ it.
     (14 hate)

L: Not anymore. Nicole and I often _____ and
                                          (15 cook)
_____ our friends for dinner on the weekends.
   (16 invite)

(continued)

M: Who _____ Nicole?
(17 be)

L: I _____ you in my last e-mail. She's my roommate.
(18 tell)

_____?
(19 you/not/remember)

M: Yes, of course. Now I _____. How could I forget?
(20 remember)

L: She's the same age as I am—19. She _____ from
(21 come)

California.

M: How _____? _____ it?
(22 be/your job) *(23 you/like)*

L: It's great! I _____ so much this summer.
(24 learn)

M: _____ you in the future?
(25 this internship/help)

L: Yes, it will. It will be great on my résumé.

M: _____ enough money?
(26 you/have)

L: No, I don't. I _____ most of the money you
(27 spend)

_____ me when I got here.
(28 give)

M: You _____ my credit card. But don't spend money on
(29 can/use)

foolish things.

L: I won't.

M: I _____ you. _____ home for a
(30 miss) *(31 you/can/come)*

weekend? We _____ for your ticket.
(32 pay)

L: I can't, Mom. We _____ activities on weekends, too.
(33 have)

M: _____ again next week?
(34 you/call)

L: If I _____ time, I _____. But I
(35 have) *(36 call)*

_____ so little free time.
(37 have)

M: I'm sure you have enough time for a ten-minute phone call to your mother.

L: You're right. I _____ you again next week. Give my
(38 call)

love to Dad.

M: I will.

Editing Advice

1. Use the correct word order for questions.

    your brother work
    Where does ~~work your brother~~?

    can't you
    Why ~~you can't~~ find a job?

    is your brother
    How old ~~your brother is~~?

2. Don't forget to use *do*, *does*, or *did* in a question.

    does your father live
    Where ~~lives your father~~?

    did   *give*
    When ˄ the teacher ~~gave~~ a test?

3. Don't use *be* with a simple present-tense or past-tense verb.

    I ~~am~~ eat breakfast every morning.

    saw
    Yesterday, he ~~was see~~ a good movie.

4. Use the base form after *do*, *does*, and *did*.

    go
    I didn't ~~went~~ to the party.

    buy
    Did you ~~bought~~ a new car?

5. For the simple present tense, use the *-s* form when the subject is
    he, *she*, *it*, or a singular noun. Use the base form in all other cases.

    s
    Lisa never drink˄ coffee in the morning.

    My friends usually visit~~s~~ me on Saturday.

6. Use the correct past form for irregular verbs.

    left
    We ~~leaved~~ the party early.

    fell
    He ~~felt~~ down on the ice.

7. Use the base form after *to*.

    drive
    I wanted to ~~drove~~ to New York.

    He likes to eat~~s~~ popcorn.

8. Use the base form after a modal.

           study
She should ~~studies~~ more.

We must ~~to~~ obey the law.

I can't help~~ing~~ you now.

9. Connect two verbs with *to* (unless one is a modal).

      to
I forgot do the homework.
      ^

      to
She needs find a job.
      ^

10. Don't use the present continuous tense with nonaction verbs.

I ~~am~~ knowing the answer now.

          s
He ~~is~~ hearing the noise in the next room.

11. Don't use *be* before a simple future verb.

The doctor will ~~be~~ see you at 3 P.M.

12. Use the correct form of *be*.

       were
They ~~was~~ late to the meeting.

      are
You ~~is~~ always on time.

13. Use the correct negative form.

       don't
They ~~not~~ know the answer.

      don't
You ~~doesn't~~ need a pen.

14. Don't forget to include a form of *be* in a present continuous sentence.

    is
She washing the dishes now.
     ^

am
I studying now.
 ^

15. Don't use the future tense in a time clause or an *if* clause. Use the simple present tense.

When I ~~will~~ graduate, I will get a job.

                             are
You will fail the course if you ~~will be~~ absent more than five times.

16. Do not use the *-ing* form for the simple present tense.

I drink~~ing~~ coffee every morning.

17. Do not forget the *-d* in *used to.*

I use to live in Mexico.
_d

18. Don't forget *to* after impersonal expressions like: *it's necessary, it's impossible, it's important.*

It's important learn English.
_{to}

Editing Quiz

Some of the shaded words and phrases have mistakes. Find the mistakes and correct them. If the shaded words are correct, write C.

A: Does your family lives in the U.S.?
(example) C   (example) live

B: Yes, but I doesn't live with them.
(1)

A: Why you don't live with them?
(2)

B: They live in Lexington. I use to live with them there, but I finded a job
(3)   (4)   (5)

here, so I was moved.
(6)

A: When you moved here?
(7)

B: Three years ago. I don't like to be so far from them, but I'm have no
(8)   (9)

choice. I didn't realized how much I would miss them. I lonely at
(10)   (11)

times, but my mom call me almost every day, so that helps.
(12)   (13)

A: I'm know how you feel. When I left home for the first time, it was very
(14)   (15)   (16)

hard for me.

B: Where your family lives?
(17)

A: They back in my country. They want visit me very much. When I
    (18)   (19)

will save enough money, I'm going to send them a plane ticket. I having
(20)   (21)   (22)

two jobs now, so soon I'll be have enough money for their trip.
                            (23)

A: How long they'll stay here?
                (24)

B: My mom can to stay for six months. She's retired. But my dad still working,
              (25)   (26)

so he can stay only for two weeks.
    (27)

A: How often do you talk to your parents?
                (28)

B: It's expensive talk by phone, so we usually send e-mail.
                (29)   (30)

A: How much costs a phone card?
                (31)

B: A phone card cost about $10, but we can only talk for about 30 minutes.
                    (32)   (33)

A: Wow. That's expensive.

B: I prefer to saving my money for their trip.
        (34)

Lesson 14 Test/Review

PART 1 **Fill in the blanks with the correct tense or form of the words in parentheses ( ).**

I _____come_____ from India. I _____ to the
      (example: come)   *(1 decide/move)*

U.S. ten months ago. It was difficult _____ my friends
                                            (2 leave)

and family, but I _____ to the U.S. and have more
                    (3 want/come)

opportunities.

   When I _____ in India, I was a draftsman. When
                (4 live)

I _____ to the U.S. in July, I _____
      (5 come)   *(6 not/find)*

a job at first because my English wasn't good enough. Last September,

I _____ a job in a restaurant. I don't like my job at all.
      (7 find)

I _____ a better job soon. I know I _____
(8 want/find)   (9 get)
a better job when I _____ English better.
                    (10 speak)
I _____ my money now. When I _____
  (11 save)   (12 have)
enough money, I _____ engineering courses at the
                (13 begin/take)
university. My parents _____ proud of me when
                       (14 be)
I _____.
  (15 graduate)
        Right now I _____ ESL courses at a college near my
                    (16 take)
house. I _____ English in India, but it was different
         (17 study)
from American English. When I listen to Americans at my job or on TV,
I _____ a lot of things they say. Sometimes when
  (18 can/not/understand)
I _____ with Americans at my job, they _____
  (19 speak)   (20 not/understand)
me. They sometimes _____ at my pronunciation. They
                    (21 laugh)
aren't bad people, but they _____ that it is hard
                            (22 not/understand)
_____ another language and live in another country.
(23 learn)
I usually _____ by myself at work. I
          (24 stay)
_____ I _____ more, but I'm very shy.
(25 know)   (26 should/practice)
        When I _____ in India, I _____
               (27 be)   (28 live)
in a big house with my parents, sisters and brothers, and grandparents.

Now I _____ a small apartment and live alone.
      (29 have)
Sometimes I _____ lonely. I would like
            (30 be)
_____ married someday, but first I want
(31 get)
_____ some money and _____
(32 earn)   (33 save)
for my future.

PART 2   **Write the negative form of the underlined words.**

EXAMPLE   He <u>moved</u> to the U.S. He ____*didn't move*____ to England.

1. He <u>studied</u> English in India. He _____ German.

2. He <u>wants to work</u> as an engineer. He _____ in a
        restaurant.

3. He <u>is going to study</u> engineering. He _____ art.

4. He <u>is taking</u> courses at a community college now. He _____ courses at a university.

5. He<u>'s saving</u> his money to get married. He _____ his money to go back to his country.

6. His coworkers <u>know</u> that he is a foreigner. They _____ how difficult his life is.

7. He <u>should</u> practice English with Americans. He _____ be shy.

8. He <u>can understand</u> some TV programs. He _____ all TV programs.

PART 3 **Read each statement. Then write a *yes/no* question about the words in parentheses ( ). Write a short answer using the words in parentheses ( ).**

EXAMPLE He studied English in India. (American English) (no)
Did he study American English? No, he didn't.

1. He'll study engineering. (accounting) (no)

   _____

2. Americans don't understand him. (Indians) (yes)

   _____

3. He's studying English now. (American English) (yes)

   _____

4. He lives in a small apartment. (with his family) (no)

   _____

5. He can understand British English well. (American English) (no)

   _____

6. It is hard to learn another language. (live in another country) (yes)

   _____

7. He wants to get married. (next year) (no)

   _____

8. He lived with his parents in India. (with his grandparents) (yes)

   _____

PART 4 Read each statement. Then write a *wh-* question with the word in parentheses ( ). An answer is not necessary.

EXAMPLE   He left India. (why)
Why did he leave India?

1. He is saving his money. (why)

2. He is going to get married. (when)

3. Some people laugh at him. (who)

4. He is lonely. (why)

5. His parents aren't in the U.S. (why)

6. He didn't find a job at first. (why)

7. He will graduate from the university. (when)

8. He came to the U.S. alone. (why)

9. His coworkers don't understand his accent. (why)

10. He lived in a big house. (when)

Expansion

Classroom

Activities

1 **Interview a student from another country. Use the words below to ask and answer questions. Practice the simple present, the present continuous, the future, and the simple past tenses.**

EXAMPLES   you/from Asia

A: Are you from Asia?

B: Yes, I am. OR No, I'm not.

where/you/from

A: Where are you from?
B: I'm from Pakistan.

a. when/you/leave your country

b. how/you/come to the U.S.

c. you/come/to the U.S. alone

d. where/you/born

e. what language(s)/you speak

f. you/return to your country next year

g. you/have a job now

h. you/have a job in your country

i. how many brothers and sisters/you/have

j. your country/big

k. your country/have a lot of problems

l. you/live in an apartment in your hometown

m. you/study English in your country

n. what/you/study this semester

o. what/you/study next semester

p. you/like this class

q. the teacher/speak your language

r. this class/hard for you

s. who/your teacher last semester

t. who/your teacher next semester

❷ Write sentences in each category, if you can. Write one for the simple present, one for the present continuous, one for the future, and one for the simple past tense.

	Simple Present	Present Continuous	Future	Simple Past
Job	I work in a factory.	I'm looking for a new job.	Next week I'm going to have an interview.	In my country, I was a taxi driver.
School				
Family				
Weather				
Apartment				

Talk

About It **❶** People often say you can't get a job without experience, and you can't get experience without a job. What do you think this means?

❷ How do you think an internship will help someone like Lena Rosen, the Washington, D.C., intern?

About It **For one of the categories in Classroom Activity 2, write a paragraph.**

EXAMPLE

My Job

I work as a taxi driver. I work six days a week.

I started this job two years ago when I came to the

U.S. It's an interesting job. I speak to my passengers.

This way, I'm learning a lot of English . . .

  For more practice using grammar in context, please visit our Web site.

Appendices

Appendix A

The Verb *GET*

Get has many meanings. Here is a list of the most common ones:

- get something = receive
  I got a letter from my father.

- get + (to) place = arrive
  I got home at six.
  What time do you get to school?

- get + object + infinitive = persuade
  She got him to wash the dishes.

- get + past participle = become

get acquainted	get worried	get hurt
get engaged	get lost	get bored
get married	get accustomed to	get confused
get divorced	get used to	get scared
get tired	get dressed	

  They got married in 1989.

- get + adjective = become

get hungry	get sleepy
get rich	get dark
get nervous	get angry
get well	get old
get upset	get fat

  It gets dark at 6:30.

- get an illness = catch
  While she was traveling, she got malaria.

- get a joke or an idea = understand
  Everybody except Tom laughed at the joke. He didn't get it.
  The boss explained the project to us, but I didn't get it.

- get ahead = advance
  He works very hard because he wants to get ahead in his job.

(continued)

- get along (well) (with someone) = have a good relationship
  She doesn't get along with her mother-in-law.
  Do you and your roommate get along well?

- get around to something = find the time to do something
  I wanted to write my brother a letter yesterday, but I didn't get around to it.

- get away = escape
  The police chased the thief, but he got away.

- get away with something = escape punishment
  He cheated on his taxes and got away with it.

- get back = return
  He got back from his vacation last Saturday.

- get back at someone = get revenge
  My brother wants to get back at me for stealing his girlfriend.

- get back to someone = communicate with someone at a later time
  The boss can't talk to you today. Can she get back to you tomorrow?

- get by = have just enough but nothing more
  On her salary, she's just getting by. She can't afford a car or a vacation.

- get in trouble = be caught and punished for doing something wrong
  They got in trouble for cheating on the test.

- get in(to) = enter a car
  She got in the car and drove away quickly.

- get out (of) = leave a car
  When the taxi arrived at the theater, everyone got out.

- get on = seat yourself on a bicycle, motorcycle, horse
  She got on the motorcycle and left.

- get on = enter a train, bus, airplane
  She got on the bus and took a seat in the back.

- get off = leave a bicycle, motorcycle, horse, train, bus, airplane
  They will get off the train at the next stop.

- get out of something = escape responsibility
  My boss wants me to help him on Saturday, but I'm going to try to get out of it.

- get over something = recover from an illness or disappointment
  She has the flu this week. I hope she gets over it soon.

- get rid of someone or something = free oneself of someone or something undesirable
  My apartment has roaches, and I can't get rid of them.

- get through (to someone) = communicate, often by telephone
  She tried to explain the harm of eating fast food to her son, but she couldn't get through to him.
  I tried to call my mother many times, but her line was busy. I couldn't get through.

- get through (with something) = finish
    I can meet you after I get through with my homework.

- get together = meet with another person
    I'd like to see you again. When can we get together?

- get up = arise from bed
    He woke up at 6:00, but he didn't get up until 6:30.

Appendix B

MAKE and DO

Some expressions use *make*. Others use *do*.

Make	Do
make a date/an appointment	do (the) homework
make a plan	do an exercise
make a decision	do the dishes
make a telephone call	do the cleaning, laundry, ironing, washing, etc.
make a reservation	do the shopping
make a meal (breakfast, lunch, dinner)	do one's best
make a mistake	do a favor
make an effort	do the right/wrong thing
make an improvement	do a job
make a promise	do business
make money	What do you do for a living? (asks about a job)
make noise	How do you do? (said when you
make the bed	meet someone for the first time)

Appendix C

Question Formation

1. Statements and Related Questions with a Main Verb

Wh- Word	Do/Does/Did (n't)	Subject	Verb	Complement
When	does	She she	watches watch	TV. TV?
Where	do	My parents your parents	live live?	in Peru.
Who(m)	does	Your sister she	likes like?	someone.
Why	did	They they	left leave	early. early?
How many books	did	She she	found find?	some books.
What kind of car	did	He he	bought buy?	a car.
Why	didn't	She she	didn't go go	home. home?
Why	doesn't	He he	doesn't like like	tomatoes. tomatoes?

Subject	Verb (base form or -s form or past form)	Complement
Someone Who	needs needs	help. help?
Someone's car Whose car	has has	problems. problems?
Someone Who	took took	my pen. my pen?
One teacher Which teacher	speaks speaks	Spanish. Spanish?
Some men Which men	have have	a car. a car?
Some boys How many boys	saw saw	the movie. the movie?
Something What	happened. happened?	

2. Statements and Related Questions with the Verb *Be*

Wh- Word	*Be*	Subject	*Be*	Complement
Where	is	She she?	is	in California.
Why	were	They they	were	hungry. hungry?
Why	isn't	He he	isn't	tired. tired?
When	was	He he	was	born in England. born?
		One student Who Which student	was was was	late. late? late?
		Some kids How many kids Which kids	were were were	afraid. afraid? afraid?

3. Statements and Related Questions with an Auxiliary (Aux) Verb and a Main Verb

Wh- Word	Aux	Subject	Aux	Main Verb	Complement
Where	is	She she	is	running. running?	
When	will	They they	will	go go	on a vacation. on a vacation?
What	should	He he	should	do do?	something.
How many pills	can	You you	can	take take?	a pill.
Why	can't	You you	can't	drive drive	a car. a car?
		Someone Who	should should	answer answer	the question. the question?

Alphabetical List of Irregular Past Forms

Base Form	Past Form	Base Form	Past Form
arise	arose	find	found
awake	awoke	fit	fit
be	was/were	flee	fled
bear	bore	fly	flew
beat	beat	forget	forgot
become	became	forgive	forgave
begin	began	freeze	froze
bend	bent	get	got
bet	bet	give	gave
bind	bound	go	went
bite	bit	grind	ground
bleed	bled	grow	grew
blow	blew	hang	hung[1]
break	broke	have	had
breed	bred	hear	heard
bring	brought	hide	hid
broadcast	broadcast	hit	hit
build	built	hold	held
burst	burst	hurt	hurt
buy	bought	keep	kept
cast	cast	kneel	knelt (or kneeled)
catch	caught	know	knew
choose	chose	lay	laid
cling	clung	lead	led
come	came	leave	left
cost	cost	lend	lent
creep	crept	let	let
cut	cut	lie	lay
deal	dealt	light	lit (or lighted)
dig	dug	lose	lost
do	did	make	made
draw	drew	mean	meant
drink	drank	meet	met
drive	drove	mistake	mistook
eat	ate	pay	paid
fall	fell	put	put
feed	fed	quit	quit
feel	felt	read	read
fight	fought	ride	rode

[1]*Hanged* is used as the past form to refer to punishment by death. *Hung* is used in other situations. She *hung* the picture on the wall.

Base Form	Past Form	Base Form	Past Form
ring	rang	stand	stood
rise	rose	steal	stole
run	ran	stick	stuck
say	said	sting	stung
see	saw	set	set
seek	sought	stink	stank
sell	sold	strike	struck
send	sent	strive	strove
forbid	forbade	swear	swore
shake	shook	sweep	swept
shed	shed	swim	swam
shine	shone (or shined)	swing	swung
shoot	shot	take	took
shrink	shrank	teach	taught
shut	shut	tear	tore
sing	sang	tell	told
sink	sank	think	thought
sit	sat	throw	threw
sleep	slept	understand	understood
slide	slid	upset	upset
slit	slit	wake	woke
speak	spoke	wear	wore
speed	sped	weave	wove
spend	spent	weep	wept
spin	spun	win	won
spit	spit (or spat)	wind	wound
split	split	withdraw	withdrew
spread	spread	wring	wrung
spring	sprang	write	wrote

Appendix E

Meanings of Modals and Related Words

- Ability, Possibility

  Can you drive a truck?
  You **can** get a ticket for speeding.

- Necessity, Obligation

  A driver **must** have a license. (legal obligation)
  I **have to** buy a new car. (personal obligation)

- Permission

  You **can** park at a meter.
  You **can't** park at a bus stop.

(continued)

- Possibility

  I **may** buy a new car soon.
  I **might** buy a Japanese car.

- Advice

  You **should** buy a new car. Your old car is in terrible condition.

- Permission Request

  May I borrow your car?
  Can I have the keys, please?
  Could I have the keys, please?

- Polite Request

  Would you teach me to drive?
  Could you show me your new car?

- Want

  What **would** you **like** to eat?
  I'**d like** a turkey sandwich.

Appendix F

Capitalization Rules

- The first word in a sentence: **My** friends are helpful.

- The word "I": My sister and **I** took a trip together.

- Names of people: Julia Roberts; George Washington

- Titles preceding names of people: Doctor (Dr.) Smith; President Lincoln; Queen Elizabeth; Mr. Rogers; Mrs. Carter

- Geographic names: the United States; Lake Superior; California; the Rocky Mountains; the Mississippi River

  NOTE: The word "the" in a geographic name is not capitalized.

- Street names: Pennsylvania Avenue (Ave.); Wall Street (St.); Abbey Road (Rd.)

- Names of organizations, companies, colleges, buildings, stores, hotels: the Republican Party; Heinle Cengage; Dartmouth College; the University of Wisconsin; the White House; Bloomingdale's; the Hilton Hotel

- Nationalities and ethnic groups: Mexicans; Canadians; Spaniards; Americans; Jews; Kurds; Eskimos

- Languages: English; Spanish; Polish; Vietnamese; Russian

- Months: January; February
- Days: Sunday; Monday
- Holidays: Christmas; Independence Day
- Important words in a title: Grammar in Context; The Old Man and the Sea; Romeo and Juliet; The Sound of Music

NOTE: Capitalize "the" as the first word of a title.

Appendix G

Metric Conversion Chart

Length

When You Know	Symbol	Multiply by	To Find	Symbol
inches	in	2.54	centimeters	cm
feet	ft	30.5	centimeters	cm
feet	ft	0.3	meters	m
yards	yd	0.91	meters	m
miles	mi	1.6	kilometers	km
Metric:				
centimeters	cm	0.39	inches	in
centimeters	cm	0.03	feet	ft
meters	m	3.28	feet	ft
meters	m	1.09	yards	yd
kilometers	km	0.62	miles	mi

Note:
12 inches = 1 foot
3 feet / 36 inches = 1 yard

Area

When You Know	Symbol	Multiply by	To Find	Symbol
square inches	in²	6.5	square centimeters	cm²
square feet	ft²	0.09	square meters	m²
square yards	yd²	0.8	square meters	m²
square miles	mi²	2.6	square kilometers	km²
Metric:				
square centimeters	cm²	0.16	square inches	in²
square meters	m²	10.76	square feet	ft²
square meters	m²	1.2	square yards	yd²
square kilometers	km²	0.39	square miles	mi²

Weight (Mass)

When You Know	Symbol	Multiply by	To Find	Symbol
ounces	oz	28.35	grams	g
pounds	lb	0.45	kilograms	kg
Metric:				
grams	g	0.04	ounces	oz
kilograms	kg	2.2	pounds	lb

Note:
1 pound = 16 ounces

Volume

When You Know	Symbol	Multiply by	To Find	Symbol
fluid ounces	fl oz	30.0	milliliters	mL
pints	pt	0.47	liters	L
quarts	qt	0.95	liters	L
gallons	gal	3.8	liters	L
Metric:				
milliliters	mL	0.03	fluid ounces	fl oz
liters	L	2.11	pints	pt
liters	L	1.05	quarts	qt
liters	L	0.26	gallons	gal

Temperature

When You Know	Symbol	Do this	To Find	Symbol
degrees Fahrenheit	°F	Subtract 32, then multiply by ⁵/₉	degrees Celsius	°C
Metric:				
degrees Celsius	°C	Multiply by ⁹/₅, then add 32	degrees Fahrenheit	°F

Sample Temperatures

Fahrenheit	Celsius
0	− 18
10	−12
20	−7
30	−1
40	4
50	10
60	16
70	21
80	27
90	32
100	38

Appendix H

Prepositions of Time

- **in** the morning: He takes a shower *in* the morning.
- **in** the afternoon: He takes a shower *in* the afternoon.
- **in** the evening: He takes a shower *in* the evening.
- **at** night: He takes a shower *at* night.

(continued)

- **in** the summer, fall, winter, spring: He takes classes *in* the summer.
- **on** that/this day: October 10 is my birthday. I became a citizen *on* that day.
- **on** the weekend: He studies *on* the weekend.
- **on** a specific day: His birthday is *on* March 5.
- **in** a month: His birthday is *in* March.
- **in** a year: He was born *in* 1978.
- **in** a century: People didn't use cars *in* the 19th century.
- **on** a day: I don't have class *on* Monday.
- **at** a specific time: My class begins *at* 12:30.
- **from** a time **to** another time: My class is *from* 12:30 *to* 3:30.
- **in** a number of hours, days, weeks, months, years: She will graduate *in* three weeks. (This means "after" three weeks.)
- **for** a number of hours, days, weeks, months, years: She was in Mexico *for* three weeks. (This means during the period of three weeks.)
- **by** a time: Please finish your test *by* six o'clock. (This means "no later than" six o'clock.)
- **until** a time: I lived with my parents *until* I came to the U.S. (This means "all the time before.")
- **during** the movie, class, meeting: He slept *during* the meeting.
- **about/around** six o'clock: The movie will begin *about* six o'clock. People will arrive *around* 5:45.
- **in** the past/future: *In* the past, she never exercised.
- **at** present: *At* present, the days are getting longer.
- **in** the beginning/end: *In* the beginning, she didn't understand the teacher at all.
- **at** the beginning/end of something: The semester begins *at* the beginning of September. My birthday is *at* the end of June.
- **before/after** a time: You should finish the job *before* Friday. The library will be closed *after* 6:00.
- **before/after** an action takes place: Turn off the lights *before* you leave. Wash the dishes *after* you finish dinner.

Glossary of Grammatical Terms

- **Adjective** An adjective gives a description of a noun.

  It's a *tall* tree.   He's an *old* man.   My neighbors are *nice*.

- **Adverb** An adverb describes the action of a sentence or an adjective or another adverb.

  She speaks English *fluently*.   I drive *carefully*.
  She speaks English *extremely* well.   She is *very* intelligent.

- **Adverb of Frequency** An adverb of frequency tells how often the action happens.

  I *never* drink coffee.   They *usually* take the bus.

- **Affirmative** means *yes*.

- **Apostrophe '** We use the apostrophe for possession and contractions.

  My *sister's* friend is beautiful.   Today *isn't* Sunday.

- **Article** The definite article is *the*. The indefinite articles are *a* and *an*.

  I have *a* cat.   I ate *an* apple.   *The* teacher came late.

- **Auxiliary Verb** Some verbs have two parts: an auxiliary verb and a main verb.

  He *can't* study.   We *will* return.

- **Base Form** The base form, sometimes called the "simple" form, of the verb has no tense. It has no ending (*-s* or *-ed*): *be, go, eat, take, write*.

  I didn't *go* out.   We don't *know* you.   He can't *drive*.

- **Capital Letter** A B C D E F G . . .

- **Clause** A clause is a group of words that has a subject and a verb. Some sentences have only one clause.

  She speaks Spanish.

Some sentences have **a main clause** and a **dependent clause**.

MAIN CLAUSE	DEPENDENT CLAUSE (**reason clause**)
She found a good job	because she has computer skills.

MAIN CLAUSE	DEPENDENT CLAUSE (**time clause**)
She'll turn off the light	before she goes to bed.

MAIN CLAUSE	DEPENDENT CLAUSE (**if clause**)
I'll take you to the doctor	if you don't have your car on Saturday.

(continued)

- **Colon** :

- **Comma** ,

- **Comparative Form** A comparative form of an adjective or adverb is used to compare two things.

  My house is *bigger* than your house.
  Her husband drives *faster* than she does.

- **Complement** The complement of the sentence is the information after the verb. It completes the verb phrase.

  He works *hard*.   I slept *for five hours*.   They are *late*.

- **Consonant** The following letters are consonants: *b, c, d, f, g, h, j, k, l, m, n, p, q, r, s, t, v, w, x, y, z.*

  NOTE: *y* is sometimes considered a vowel, as in the world *syllable*.

- **Contraction** A contraction is made up of two words put together with an apostrophe.

  He's my brother.   *You're* late.   They *won't* talk to me.
  (*He's* = he is)   (*You're* = you are)   (*won't* = will not)

- **Count Noun** Count nouns are nouns that we can count. They have a singular and a plural form.

  1 pen – 3 pens   1 table – 4 tables

- **Dependent Clause** See **Clause**.

- **Direct Object** A direct object is a noun (phrase) or pronoun that receives the action of the verb.

  We saw *the movie*.   You have *a nice car*.   I love *you*.

- **Exclamation Mark** !

- **Frequency Words** Frequency words are *always, usually, generally, often, sometimes, rarely, seldom, hardly ever, never.*

  I *never* drink coffee.   We *always* do our homework.

- **Hyphen** –

- **Imperative** An imperative sentence gives a command or instructions. An imperative sentence omits the word *you*.

  Come here.   *Don't be* late.   Please *sit* down.

- **Infinitive** An infinitive is *to* + base form.

  I want *to leave*.   You need *to be* here on time.

- **Linking Verb** A linking verb is a verb that links the subject to the noun or adjective after it. Linking verbs include *be, seem, feel, smell, sound, look, appear, taste.*

  She *is* a doctor.   She *seems* very intelligent.   She *looks* tired.

- **Modal** The modal verbs are *can, could, shall, should, will, would, may, might, must.*

  They *should* leave.   I *must* go.

- **Negative** means no.

- **Nonaction Verb** A nonaction verb has no action. We do not use a continuous tense (*be* + verb *-ing*) with a nonaction verb. The nonaction verbs are: *believe, cost, care, have, hear, know, like, love, matter, mean, need, own, prefer, remember, see, seem, think, understand, want,* and sense-perception verbs.

  She *has* a laptop.   We *love* our mother.   You *look* great.

- **Noncount Noun** A noncount noun is a noun that we don't count. It has no plural form.

  She drank some *water*.   He prepared some *rice*.
  Do you need any *money*?   We had a lot of *homework*.

- **Noun** A noun is a person (*brother*), a place (*kitchen*), or a thing (*table*). Nouns can be either count (*1 table, 2 tables*) or noncount (*money, water*).

  My *brother* lives in California.   My *sisters* live in New York.
  I get *advice* from them.   I drink *coffee* every day.

- **Noun Modifier** A noun modifier makes a noun more specific.

  fire department   *Independence* Day   *can* opener

- **Noun Phrase** A noun phrase is a group of words that form the subject or object of the sentence.

  A *very nice woman* helped me at registration.
  I bought *a big box of cereal*.

- **Object** The object of the sentence follows the verb. It receives the action of the verb.

  He bought *a car*.   I saw *a movie*.   I met *your brother*.

- **Object Pronoun** Use object pronouns (*me, you, him, her, it, us, them*) after the verb or preposition.

  He likes *her*.   I saw the movie. Let's talk about *it*.

- **Parentheses** ( )

- **Paragraph** A paragraph is a group of sentences about one topic.

- **Participle, Present** The present participle is verb + *-ing*.

  She is *sleeping*.   They were *laughing*.

- **Period** .

- **Phrase** A group of words that go together.

  Last month my sister came to visit.
  There is a strange car *in front of my house*.

(continued)

- **Plural** Plural means more than one. A plural noun usually ends with -s.

    She has beautiful *eyes*.   My *feet* are big.

- **Possessive Form** Possessive forms show ownership or relationship.

    Mary's coat is in the closet.   My *brother* lives in Miami.

- **Preposition** A preposition is a short connecting word: *about, above, across, after, around, as, at, away, back, before, behind, below, by, down, for, from, in, into, like, of, off, on, out, over, to, under, up, with.*

    The book is *on* the table.   She studies *with* her friends.

- **Pronoun** A pronoun takes the place of a noun.

    I have a new car. I bought *it* last week.
    John likes Mary, but *she* doesn't like *him*.

- **Punctuation** Period . Comma , Colon : Semicolon ; Question Mark ? Exclamation Mark !

- **Question Mark** ?

- **Quotation Marks** " "

- **Regular Verb** A regular verb forms its past tense with -ed.

    He *worked* yesterday.   I *laughed* at the joke.

- **-s Form** A present tense verb that ends in -s or -es.

    He *lives* in New York.   She *watches* TV a lot.

- **Sense-Perception Verb** A sense-perception verb has no action. It describes a sense. The sense perception verbs are: *look, feel, taste, sound, smell.*

    She *feels* fine.   The coffee *smells* fresh.   The milk *tastes* sour.

- **Sentence** A sentence is a group of words that contains a subject[2] and a verb (at least) and gives a complete thought.

    SENTENCE: She came home.
    NOT A SENTENCE: When she came home

- **Simple Form of Verb** The simple form of the verb, also called the base form, has no tense; it never has an -s, -ed, or -ing ending.

    Did you *see* the movie?   I couldn't *find* your phone number.

- **Singular** Singular means one.

    She ate a *sandwich*.   I have one *television*.

- **Subject** The subject of the sentence tells who or what the sentence is about.

    My *sister* got married last April. *The wedding* was beautiful.

---

[2]In an imperative sentence, the subject *you* is omitted: *Sit down. Come here.*

- **Subject Pronouns** Use subject pronouns (*I, you, he, she, it, we, you, they*) before a verb.

  They speak Japanese.   *We* speak Spanish.

- **Superlative Form** A superlative form of an adjective or adverb shows the number one item in a group of three or more.

  January is the *coldest* month of the year.
  My brother speaks English the *best* in my family.

- **Syllable** A syllable is a part of a word that has only one vowel sound. (Some words have only one syllable.)

  change (one syllable)   after (af·ter = two syllables)
  look (one syllable)   responsible (re·spon·si·ble = four syllables)

- **Tag Question** A tag question is a short question at the end of a sentence. It is used in conversation.

  You speak Spanish, *don't you?*   He's not happy, *is he?*

- **Tense** A verb has tense. Tense shows when the action of the sentence happened.

  SIMPLE PRESENT: She usually *works* hard.
  FUTURE: She *will work* tomorrow.
  PRESENT CONTINUOUS: She *is working* now.
  SIMPLE PAST: She *worked* yesterday.

- **Verb** A verb is the action of the sentence.

  He *runs* fast.   I *speak* English.

  Some verbs have no action. They are linking verbs. They connect the subject to the rest of the sentence.

  He *is* tall.   She *looks* beautiful.   You *seem* tired.

- **Vowel** The following letters are vowels: *a, e, i, o, u*. *Y* is sometimes considered a vowel (for example, in the word *mystery*).

Appendix J

Verbs and Adjectives Followed by a Preposition

(be) accustomed to	forgive someone for	(be) proud of
(be) afraid of	(be) glad about	recover from
agree with	(be) good at	(be) related to
(be) angry about	(be) happy about	rely on/upon
(be) angry at/with	hear about	(be) responsible for
approve of	hear of	(be) sad about
argue about	hope for	(be) satisfied with
(be) ashamed of	(be) incapable of	(be) scared of
(be) aware of	insist on/upon	(be) sick of
believe in	(be) interested in	(be) sorry about
(be) bored with/by	(be) involved in	(be) sorry for
(be) capable of	(be) jealous of	speak about
care about/for	(be) known for	speak to/with
(be) compared to	(be) lazy about	succeed in
complain about	listen to	(be) sure of/about
(be) concerned about	look at	(be) surprised at
concentrate on	look for	take care of
consist of	look forward to	talk about
count on	(be) mad about	talk to/with
deal with	(be) mad at	thank someone for
decide on	(be) made from/of	(be) thankful to someone for
depend on/upon	(be) married to	think about/of
dream about/of	object to	(be) tired of
(be) engaged to	participate in	(be) upset about
(be) excited about	plan on	(be) upset with
(be) familiar with	pray to	(be) used to
(be) famous for	pray for	wait for
feel like	(be) prepared for	warn about
(be) fond of	prohibit someone from	(be) worried about
forget about	protect someone from	worry about

Appendix K

Map of the United States of America

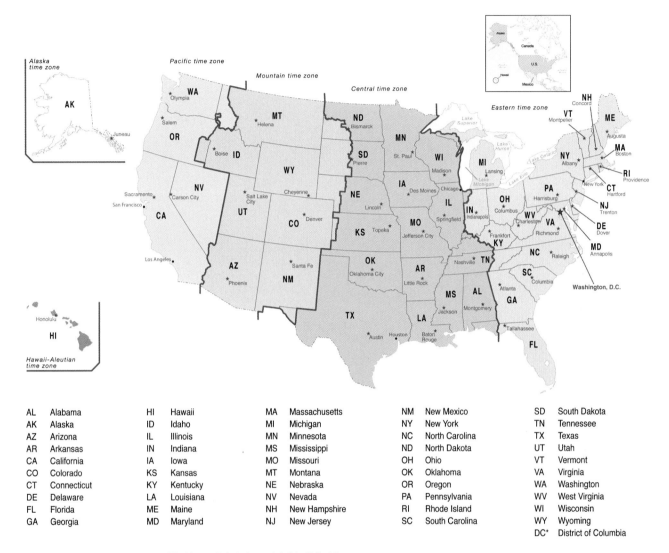

AL	Alabama	HI	Hawaii	MA	Massachusetts	NM	New Mexico	SD	South Dakota
AK	Alaska	ID	Idaho	MI	Michigan	NY	New York	TN	Tennessee
AZ	Arizona	IL	Illinois	MN	Minnesota	NC	North Carolina	TX	Texas
AR	Arkansas	IN	Indiana	MS	Mississippi	ND	North Dakota	UT	Utah
CA	California	IA	Iowa	MO	Missouri	OH	Ohio	VT	Vermont
CO	Colorado	KS	Kansas	MT	Montana	OK	Oklahoma	VA	Virginia
CT	Connecticut	KY	Kentucky	NE	Nebraska	OR	Oregon	WA	Washington
DE	Delaware	LA	Louisiana	NV	Nevada	PA	Pennsylvania	WV	West Virginia
FL	Florida	ME	Maine	NH	New Hampshire	RI	Rhode Island	WI	Wisconsin
GA	Georgia	MD	Maryland	NJ	New Jersey	SC	South Carolina	WY	Wyoming
								DC*	District of Columbia

*The District of Columbia is not a state. Washington, D.C., is the capital of the United States.
Note: Washington, D.C., and Washington state are not the same.

Index

A

A/an, 114–115
  before adjectives, 332
  with count nouns, 313
  before definitions, 11
  for generalizations about subject, 117
  with indefinite nouns, 114
  vs. *some*, 313
Ability, *can* to express, 275, 403
Action verbs, 172, 173
Adjectives, 331, 332
  vs. adverbs of manner, 337
  articles before, 332
  following *be*, 9
  comparative, 356–357, 363
  in definitions, 11
  to describe nouns, 331, 332
  ending with –*ed*, 332
  ending with –*ing*, 332, 335
  enough with, 342
  following *how*, 25
  infinitives following, 266
  one or *ones* substituted for nouns with, 332
  possessive, 133
  same form as adverbs, 337
  comma with, 332
  superlative, 356–357, 358, 360
  too before, 344
  very before, 9
  word order with superlative, 360
  word order with comparative, 365
Adverbs, 331
  comparative, 356–357, 365
  enough with, 342
  following *how*, 25
  of manner, 331, 337
  same as adjectives, 337
  superlative, 356–357, 360
  too before, 344
  between *will* and main verb, 191
  word order with superlatives, 331, 360
  word order with comparatives, 365
Advice, *should* to give or ask for, 277
Advisability, *should* to express, 403
A *few*
  with count nouns, 312
  vs. *a little*, 312
Affirmative questions
  with *be*, 24, 231, 406

with *be going to*, 198, 406
with *future* tense, 198–199, 406
with modals, 273, 406
with present continuous tense, 164, 405
with simple past tense, 231, 243, 406
with simple present tense, 59, 405
with *will*, 199, 406
Affirmative statements
  with *be*, 24, 45, 231
  with *be going to*, 198
  with future tense, 406
  with modals, 273
  much versus *a lot of* in, 311
  with negative tag questions, 380
  with present continuous tense, 164, 405
  with simple past tense, 231, 243, 406
  with simple present tense, 59, 405
    of *be* and other verbs, compared, 45
    questions compared with, 51
  with *will*, 199
Age, simple past tense of *be* with, 230
Ago, 225
A *little*
  with comparatives, 363
  with noncount nouns, 312
  vs. *a few*, 312
A *lot*, 311
A *lot of*, 311, 318
  with count and noncount nouns, 311
  vs. *much*, 311
Any, 114–115
  with count and noncount nouns, 313
  with indefinite nouns, 115
  following negative verbs, 313
  vs. *no*, 313
  vs. *some*, 313
Apostrophe (')
  in contractions, 8
  in possessive nouns, 131
Articles. *See A/an; The*
Auxiliary verbs
  in American and British English, 46, 51, 377
  with opposite statements, 376
  in short answers, 20, 51, 59, 164, 198–199, 231, 243, 384
  following subject pronouns in comparisons, 361

in tag questions, 379, 380–381
with *too* and *either*, 374, 375

B

Base form
  with future, 191, 192
  in infinitives, 262
  with imperatives, 286
  after modals, 273
  with *let's*, 289
  with simple past tense, 225
  with simple present tense, 41
Be
  affirmative statements with, 24
    other verbs compared with, 45
  as auxiliary verb, 377
  with *born*, 230, 253, 403
  with location, 4
  classifications, *be* with
    simple past tense, 230
    simple present tense, 4, 11, 403
  contractions of, 8
    negative, 15, 24, 159
    in short answers, 20
    simple past tense, 229
    with subject pronoun and *be*, 8, 159
  frequency words with, word order with, 78
  negative statements with, 15, 229, 231
    other verbs compared with, 48
  with present continuous tense, 159
  questions with
    negative, 24, 231
    simple past tense in, 231
    wh- questions, 21–22, 63
    yes/no questions, 20, 54
  in short answers, 20
  simple past tense of, 228, 229, 406
    with definitions or classifications, 230
    with descriptions, 230
    negative statements with, 229
    questions with, 231
  simple present tense of, 2, 54, 63, 406
    in affirmative statements, 45
    contractions with, 7, 8, 229
    with definitions or classifications, 4, 11, 403
    with descriptions, 4, 9, 403
    forms of, 3

Photo Credits